NIGEL MANSELL'S
Indy Car Racing

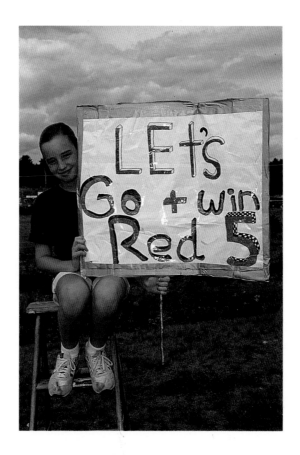

NIGEL MANSELL'S
Indy Car Racing

Nigel Mansell

and Jeremy Shaw

Photographs by John Townsend

Weidenfeld and Nicolson
London

© Nigel Mansell and George Weidenfeld & Nicolson Ltd 1993

First published in 1993 by George Weidenfeld & Nicolson Ltd
Orion House, 5 Upper St Martin's Lane, London WC2H 9EA

British Library Cataloguing-in Publication data

A catalogue record for this book is available from the British Library

ISBN 0 297 83249 2

Design by Behram Kapadia

Typeset by Selwood Systems, Midsomer Norton
Colour separations by Newsele Litho
Printed and bound in Great Britain by Butler & Tanner Ltd, Frome and London

Contents

This book is dedicated to all the sponsors and fans around the world, but especially to Carl Haas and Paul Newman, who have opened the doors to a brand new adventure in Indy cars.

Transition from Formula 1 to Indy

*I*ndy Car racing is a unique form of motorsport. There are undoubtedly some comparisons which can be drawn with Formula 1, notably in that they both feature high-performance open-wheel single-seater cars propelled by engines which produce around 750 horsepower; but in reality the similarities end there. The cars require a different driving technique and they are driven on different types of track.

Even in my relatively brief experience of the Indy Car scene I have come to appreciate the tremendous versatility that is involved. The sport requires very special skills. You just have to examine – or preferably visit – a few of the races to realize how true that is. Indianapolis itself is quite unique, totally unlike any other race track in the world. In addition, the blend of super-speedways, short ovals, street circuits and natural road courses ensures the series is a constant challenge. In order to mount a serious threat for the PPG Cup championship you have to be competitive in each discipline.

I think that goes some way towards explaining why Indy Car racing has always interested me. In the past, however, Formula 1 has kept me more than busy. For thirteen years it was my life, and my family and I were totally consumed by it.

But over the course of the last few years I have to admit there were certain aspects of Formula 1 that were getting me down. Especially the politics. I am not a political person. I'm a family man and a racing driver. I like to think I handle both 'jobs' quite satisfactorily. But a politician I am not.

I don't really want to go into all the details of why I moved to Indy Car racing, but suffice to say I don't think I was treated very well late in the 1992 Formula 1 season. From the human point of view, after putting my heart and soul into my job, which I've done throughout my whole career, I didn't expect to be treated as shabbily as I was – especially after taking fourteen poles, winning nine races, gaining numerous world records and finally attaining my goal of winning the Formula 1 World Championship.

Much the same goes, I should say, for my former teammate Riccardo Patrese who is a great driver and is also the most experienced driver in Formula 1. Yet, he was fired at the end of the year.

Opposite Second place in the Hungarian Grand Prix was enough to clinch the Formula 1 World Championship in 1992.

There was a time when I thought I had a deal on the table for 1993, one that would have given me the opportunity to defend my world championship in the same manner I was afforded in winning it. Then I was told everything had changed. In fact there was a period of about three weeks when, basically, I had to make a choice between two alternatives: I could go to a lesser team or retire.

I wasn't ready for either of those scenarios. The prospect of winning has always been my motivator. That's why I do what I do. I'm in it to win, nothing less. In Formula 1, I had worked hard to develop the car and the engine and various other components to the point where the entire package was capable of winning races on a consistent basis. That's how I was able to win the World Championship – with a great deal of help from a lot of other people who worked equally hard at Williams and Renault.

As far as I was concerned, there were many benefits which remained to be reaped. So I wasn't ready to retire. Not yet.

I know I had been quoted in the past as saying I'd probably retire if, and when, I won the world championship, but I have an easy explanation. I admit I did say that, but I did so primarily to shut people up. I just got so fed up with being asked what I'd do if I won the world championship; and rather than talk to people about it – because things like that are very private, very personal – I just gave them a final answer. It's not the sort of thing

Outwardly my Lola-Ford/Cosworth Indy car (*right*) looks quite similar to the Formula 1 Williams-Renault I raced in 1992 (*below*). But the Lola is almost 400 lbs heavier and runs on smaller tyres. It has a turbocharged engine and a manual gearbox.

anyone wants to discuss in public. When the time comes to retire, that'll be it; but up until then I want to keep those thoughts to myself.

By saying what I did, I stopped people asking me any more questions. At times I do say throw-away lines that are specifically aimed to shut people up because otherwise they start pontificating: well, what if you do this, you do that, you do the other? What-if? What-if? What-if? And to be quite honest I don't want to talk to the sort of people who only want to know things like that all the time. Equally I don't want to fall out with them, and you can't just say, 'I'm not telling you.' I decided it was better to say something, so I said: 'I'll probably pack it up.' And that was it.

What it all boils down to is the fact I still wanted to go racing. And I wanted to win and felt I could still win. There is no question whatsoever that if I had been given the opportunity to defend the world championship in the manner in which I won it, then I would have stayed in Formula 1. But by late August 1992 it had become apparent that that wouldn't be the case.

It was then that I received a telephone call from Carl Haas. If you're not familiar with Carl, he's one of the most influential people in North American motorsport. He used to race himself in the '50s, purely as an amateur, but once he made the switch to being a team owner he never looked back. He's won just about everything there is to win. His team started out in Formula 5000 – a great, though now-defunct, category with single-seater chassis and big, powerful 5-litre V8 engines – and won everything in sight, mainly with another Englishman, Brian Redman, as his driver.

Haas was equally successful in the thundering Can-Am series, which was reborn in 1977 after pricing itself out of the market a few years earlier. Haas

Below Carl Haas invariably 'wears' a huge cigar and is an obsessive backgammon player. He's a racer. He doesn't like to lose. At anything.

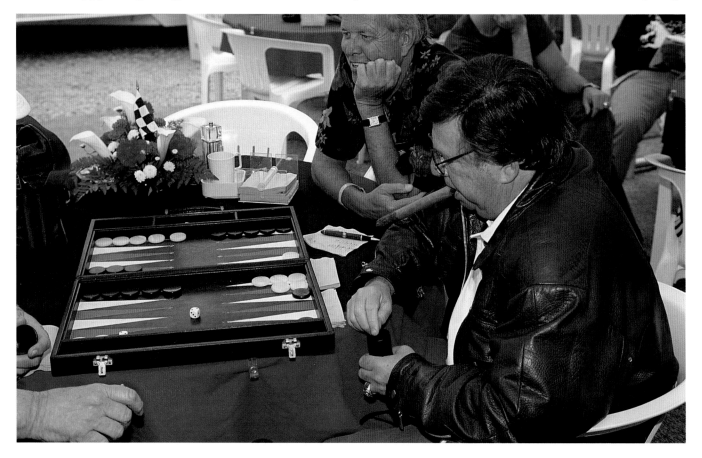

Right Carl's partner, Paul Newman, is a gentleman and a sportsman. Here he offers a word of encouragement at Milwaukee.

effectively emulated the great McLaren team of Bruce McLaren and Denny Hulme – 'The Bruce and Denny Show' – which totally dominated the scene in the late 1960s and early '70s. Grand Prix driver Patrick Tambay took over the drive when Redman was injured in a crash at St Jovite, Canada, and won the title quite easily in 1977. Fellow Formula 1 drivers Alan Jones and Jacky Ickx followed suit in the next two seasons, with Tambay returning to sweep up again in 1980.

All the while, Carl was importing all sorts of British racing cars and accessories into the States. He was the sole concessionaire for Lola and Crossle, selling literally hundreds of Formula Ford cars in the 1970s. He also marketed Hewland transmissions among other much-needed components. In short, he became an extremely successful businessman.

In 1984, Carl effectively merged his team with famed film actor and self-proclaimed racing car nut Paul Newman. The result was Newman-Haas Racing. Paul, who, incidentally, is an accomplished racing driver in his own right, had been competing against Haas as a rival owner in the Can-Am series. Both wanted to move up into the Indy Car ranks. So, at Carl's instigation, they did. Together.

Today, Carl has his fingers in many pies. Aside from running his import business and his racing team, he's on the board of governors for Indy Car Inc., the sanctioning body for Indy Car racing, and is Chairman of the Board of the Sports Car Club of America, which caters primarily for the clubman and is the largest racing club in the world with around 50,000 members. He's a race promoter, too, staging events on the famed Milwaukee Mile oval, and is on the Board of Directors at Road America, a four-mile road course almost universally regarded as the most scenic and challenging in North America.

Carl Haas is not an imposing man, as you might expect for someone as important as he. In fact he's quite short. He dresses well and *always* has a huge cigar in his mouth. He speaks sparingly – and with a voice so quiet it's almost a whisper; but when he talks, you listen. Above, all, though, he's a racer, and in many ways, though obviously very different ways, he reminds me of Lotus's Colin Chapman, who gave me my first Formula 1 opportunity in 1986. I've got an enormous amount of respect for both of them.

Incredibly, given his vast array of vested interests, Carl, while widely envied, has hardly any foes. He has worked hard for his spoils and earned a reputation as a thoroughly honourable character. If Carl says something, he means it. You can hold him to his word.

That is certainly an accurate assessment of my dealings with him. And with Paul Newman, who, like Carl, called me several times during those weeks in which I had to make a decision about my future.

Below My good friend Greg Norman and Rosanne look concerned during the race at Surfers Paradise. We won but it was far from plain sailing.

Right My family is much more a part of the scene in America. Leo, Greg and Chloe celebrate with me on the victory podium at Milwaukee.

In actual fact, it wasn't the first time Carl and I had sat in deep conversation on opposite ends of the telephone line. A couple of years ago, when Indy Car star Michael Andretti first started sniffing seriously at Formula 1, Carl and I talked about the possibility of me racing in the States. At the time, of course, it wasn't possible. I was too committed to Formula 1. But the link had been made. We talked and we explored each other's ideas and thoughts. We seemed to be on the same wavelength right away.

So, when Michael Andretti had finally made it known to Carl that he was going to make the jump into Formula 1, Carl and Paul needed a driver. I was the first person they called.

In reality it didn't take long for me – or rather, my wife Rosanne and I, the Mansell Team as we call it – to make the decision to go with Carl and Paul. We had to do some soul-searching, because, as I say, Formula 1 had been our life for the past thirteen years, but really it wasn't too difficult. And the nice thing for me is that I can look anybody straight between the eyes and say that before we agreed anything with Carl, I'd left Formula 1 – for the right reasons – and it was about ten days later that we actually came to a decision to do something in Indy Car racing. Again, it was basically because of Carl that it happened. Without his tenacity and perseverance and understanding, there's no way I would be doing what I am now. He, together with Paul and our family of sponsors, including Kmart, Texaco and Ford Motor Company, created the situation and made it all possible. They gave me the motivation. Collectively they wanted to go racing – and at the same time have some fun.

I know some journalists didn't reflect the fact, particularly during the 1992 season, but I love nothing more than racing – other than my family, of course, and maybe the odd round of golf. I had the best year of my career in '92. I drove some of my finest races; and who knows, it might have been even better if I hadn't been punted off a few times!

Seriously, though, the racing does seem to be a lot more enjoyable in America. It's tough, it's extremely competitive, but everyone has fun at the same time. Our Newman-Haas team is like one big happy family. They're a fabulous bunch, through and through. The blend of people, the calibre of people, is second to none. There is no doubt in my mind that the Newman-Haas team ranks right up alongside Williams and McLaren and Ferrari. No question about it. Their organization, the skills of the people within the team, is totally parallel to Formula 1 as far as I'm concerned.

The same goes for our sponsors. The other teams, too. Everybody talks to one another, from the owners to the mechanics. The egos seem to be kept very much under control.

The whole ambience of the Indy Car scene is superb. Bobby Rahal, the defending PPG Indy Car World Series champion, is a great driver and a great ambassador for the sport. So's my own teammate Mario Andretti. He's a giant among men – figuratively if not literally. The same goes for Emerson Fittipaldi, Danny Sullivan, Al Unser Jr. and a host of others. There are some great champions, and they know they're not bigger than the sport. Quite honestly, it's a marked contrast to the world from which I came, where some of the drivers seem to think the sport wouldn't survive without them. Little do they know . . .

Above I play golf whenever I get the chance.

Opposite above Bobby Rahal had a torrid time in the early part of the season. He tried to develop his own Rahal/Hogan chassis, an updated version of the car run in 1992 by the Truesports team, but after failing to qualify at Indianapolis he made the decision to switch to a customer Lola.

Right Mario Andretti offers some advice: 'Nothin' to it, Nigel, just follow me'.

The Evolution of Indy Racing

'The Brickyard' as it was in 1936. Eventual winner Louis Meyer isn't even in the picture on the parade lap. He started 28th but came through to become the first three-time Indianapolis 500 winner. He also took home the Packard 120 Convertible pace car.

*W*hat does the Indianapolis Motor Speedway have in common with the Silverstone Grand Prix circuit? About as much, perhaps, as the White House in Washington, D.C., shares with the House of Commons in London – insofar as the two race tracks, politically speaking, represent the power-house of motor racing in North America and England respectively.

Silverstone, which is billed as 'The Home of British Motor Racing', has come to be regarded as one of the world's classic road racing venues. It might be no match for the old Nurburgring or the original Spa-Francorchamps in terms of the challenge it presents to the drivers – although sadly I never had the opportunity to race on either of those two grand old circuits – nor perhaps can it boast the fanatical spectator following at Monza. (Now I think of it though, after witnessing some of the scenes at Silverstone first-hand in the last few British Grands Prix, I'm not quite so sure about that.) Anyway, Silverstone, apart from being one of my favourite circuits, has established a niche of its own in the Grand Prix racing calendar. It is traditionally one of the best-attended and best-organized races of the season, held on a circuit that comprises a superb blend of fast and medium-fast corners.

Indianapolis is rather different, to put it mildly. It is grandly proclaimed as 'The Greatest Race Course in the World', and I, for one, am not going to argue with that description. For starters, it redefines the term 'fast'. When we talk about a fast corner in Europe, we think of the old Stowe and Club at Silverstone, or perhaps Signes at Paul Ricard, at the end of the long Mistrale straight. But none even comes close to the mind-boggling speeds at Indianapolis, where the drivers – even those in the slowest cars – have to commit themselves to turning left into a blind corner, with a very solid-looking concrete wall and a huge, high debris fence just a few inches away from the right-side wheels, at 240-odd miles per hour. It's an incredible experience, one of the most daunting I've ever encountered in a racing car.

Amazingly, though, if you look back into the history of Silverstone and Indianapolis, they share the same roots. And those roots stem from the human race's innate desire to compete. To win. To be the best. To prove to the world that one particular product – or one person – is better than any other.

It was the same for those who produced cars or those who drove them; and it was a natural progression in the very early years of the automobile, almost 100 years ago, that cars and drivers would compete against one another.

The first acknowledged race – although officially it was called a 'Trial' since outright speed was not the sole factor used in determining the winner – was held in France in July, 1894, over public 'roads' (which in truth were little more than rough, dusty cart tracks) between Paris and Rouen, a distance of around 79 miles. It was 'won' at an average speed of 11.6 mph. A few months later, inspired by the publicity gained by the French pioneers, the Chicago Times-Herald newspaper hosted an event in North America, with competitors 'racing' from Chicago to Evanston, Illinois, and back. The solitary finisher covered the 54 miles at a meagre average of 6.5 mph.

Above Silverstone, 1992. The ultimate patriotism?

The next few years saw a proliferation of city-to-city races on both sides of the Atlantic Ocean. Gradually the sport evolved into a more organized endeavour, thanks in no small part to the efforts of an American newspaper magnate, James Gordon Bennett.

A resident of Paris at the turn of the century, Bennett was largely responsible for the 'modernization' of our sport. He drew up the first set of rules to govern both the cars and the way in which races were run. Many of them, including a development of his system of warning flags, are still in use today.

The sophistication of the cars increased rapidly. So did the speeds. And accidents became more common. In 1903, a much-vaunted race between Paris and Madrid was tragically curtailed by a series of crashes, one of which claimed the life of Marcel Renault, one of the founders of the French manufacturing giant and one of the first true champions of the fledgling sport of motor racing. Horrified by the adverse publicity, the French government ordered the race to be stopped. An era was at an end.

But the competitive spirit endured. People soon realized that closed-course events provided a far more acceptable format, and even though most continued to be held over public roads, thanks to the farsightedness of Gordon Bennett they were now properly supervised to prevent un-authorized access.

Right Flag-waving of an entirely different kind: a marshal displays crossed yellow flags, signifying a full-course caution. This procedure owes its roots to the foresight of Gordon Bennett.

Once again, American influence helped to perpetuate the genre. In 1904, another wealthy publisher, William K. Vanderbilt Jr., established the first of a series of races within easy reach of his native New York City. The inaugural Vanderbilt Cup race was held over 284 miles on a course starting and finishing in Westbury on Long Island. Almost immediately the event attracted vast crowds and had a strong international flavour.

The 1906 race drew such an enormous throng of spectators, estimated at half a million, that the event was in danger of becoming a victim of its own success. There was just no obvious way to control the crowds. After cancelling the race in 1907, however, Vanderbilt came to the rescue once more, using long sections of his self-financed Long Island Motor Parkway for the closed-course events which continued from 1908 through 1910.

By this stage another option had become available: shorter circuits run on private land. The first such race known to have taken place was also in America, on a one-mile oval at the Rhode Island State Fair at Cranston, Rhode Island, in 1896.

It took a while for the concept to catch on, but when the world's first purpose-built race track was opened in 1907, it was done so in a country previously bereft of any form of motorized competition: in England.

Our British forebears had been slow to respond to the growing import-ance of the automobile. Indeed in the very early years a law was passed which required any moving car to be preceded by a man carrying a red flag. Even ten years after this patently ludicrous demand was repealed in 1896, racing on public roads continued to be outlawed; but then a wealthy landowner in Surrey came up with a solution. In collaboration with a group of enthusiasts, H. F. (Hugh) Locke-King produced plans for a race track on which British manufacturers could test and develop their machines. Thus was Brooklands born.

Countless legends have been spawned by the vast pear-shaped 'oval', where imposing banked turns dominated the 2.75-mile layout. Over the next thirty years or so Brooklands became synonymous with speed. A host of records were established on the concrete bankings. But once more Britain was destined to lag behind the rest of the world. Some of the races at Brooklands were run on a handicap basis, following precisely the format of horse racing events. Furthermore it soon became an extremely exclusive club for the enjoyment of the upper classes. The Brooklands motto said it all: 'The Right Crowd And No Crowding'.

What a contrast it was to the world's second purpose-built race track: the Indianapolis Motor Speedway.

Oval track racing had already caught on in America, primarily on dirt tracks used hitherto for horses. They provided a perfect venue, with spec-tators housed easily and in relative comfort. The tracks themselves tended to produce close racing and plenty of thrills and spills in the true American spirit. Race promotion soon became quite a lucrative business.

One such promoter was a gentleman by the name of Carl Fisher who lived in the midwestern town of Indianapolis, Indiana, an important centre of the motor industry. We'll go into the development and growth of the Fisher-inspired Indianapolis Motor Speedway a little later on, but suffice to say it soon spawned a rapid growth of motor racing in America, especially on oval-track layouts.

Above Early in 1904, William K. Vanderbilt Jr. bettered the existing land speed record when he achieved 92.30 mph in a Mercedes at Ormond Beach, Florida. Strangely, his standard was never officially recognized by the Europeans.

The first race (actually for motorcycles) on Fisher's 2.5-mile speedway, which featured a surface of crushed stone and tar, was held in August of 1909. It was a fiasco. The track broke up terribly. A decision soon was made to re-cover the entire length with bricks – hence the 'Brickyard' moniker which has endured to this day, even though the bricks have long since been paved over with asphalt.

At around the same time, another form of race track sprang to prominence, again uniquely, in North America. The birth of the motor car (or automobile as it is still predominantly referred to in the US) had, of course, been preceded by the bicycle. And, given the propensity for competition, bicycle race tracks – called velodromes – had become popular. Constructed from relatively inexpensive two-by-four pine 'boards' and featuring steep banking, the tracks fostered close competition and handlebar-to-handlebar action.

So, a couple of California engineers, Fred Moscovics, who went on to head the Stutz Motor Company, and Jack Prince, decided to apply the same construction techniques in building a similar track specifically for car racing. The first 'motordrome' was completed just outside Los Angeles, California, at Playa del Rey, in 1909. Over the next twenty years, many more board tracks, as they became known, were built around the country. They were fearsomely fast, due mainly to the steep banking which reached as much as 45 degrees. In June of 1915, cheered on by no fewer than 80,000 spectators, Italian-born English-raised Dario Resta took his Peugeot to victory in a 500-mile race on 'the boards' at the two-mile Maywood Speedway in Chicago. His winning average speed was an impressive 97.5 mph. A couple of months later, Resta stormed to the chequered flag in a 100-mile race on the same track at an average of 101.8 mph.

The sport by now had really taken a strong hold in America. Races all over the country, including the early Vanderbilt Cup events, were staged by the American Automobile Association (the 'Triple-A' and the equivalent of our own AA in England), which also was invited to sanction the inaugural Indianapolis 500 in 1911. A championship series represented the next logical progression.

Historians, however, disagree upon when the first true championship was held. In reality, the official AAA National Championship began in 1916, with Resta proclaimed as a worthy champion after winning five times, including by far the most prestigious race on the calendar – a 300-mile affair (shortened out of respect for the war in Europe) at Indianapolis. It was the only time the event has been scheduled for less than 500 miles.

The Great War precluded any more official championship racing until 1920, when, once again, AAA records become confused. At the beginning of the year, eleven events were apparently on the schedule. Proper computation of the point scoring procedure would have placed Tommy Milton as champion. At season's end, though, only five races were listed, with Indianapolis 500 winner Gaston Chevrolet shown atop the point standings.

But the confusion doesn't begin or end there. Modern Indy Car records credit George Robertson with winning the first championship in 1909. In fact, early race statistics were compiled by the editors at *Motor Age* magazine, who in that year saw fit to determine Robertson as their own first National Driving Champion. Then, in 1926 and 1927, Val Haresnape, secretary of

Below Simplex driver George Robertson was credited with winning the first AAA National Championship.

the AAA contest board, and associate Arthur Means began to reconstruct 'official' championship records pertaining to the years 1909–20, based on a variety of AAA-sanctioned events. These listings seem to have been ignored by the sanctioning body at the time, only to be 'rediscovered' in 1952, since when they have become regarded as historically correct.

Needless to say, Indy Car racing – indeed the sport as a whole – has progressed immeasurably since those early days. Even so, while those in charge might seem, with hindsight, not to have been in total control, there was no lack of intensity or commitment among the competitors themselves. In 1919, qualifying speeds at Indianapolis reached over 100 mph for the first time, with Rene Thomas, who had won the race in 1914, claiming the pole at a new record of 104.78 mph in his French-built Ballot.

In those pioneer years, cars imported from Europe – such as Ballot, Delage, Fiat, Peugeot and Mercedes – tended to dominate the scene, not only because most of the American challengers tended to be lightly modified production cars, but more specifically because racing in continental Europe had already reached quite sophisticated levels.

It was much the same story regarding drivers. Resta, Thomas, Jules Goux and Georges Boillot were among those who travelled to America in search of a share in the winnings, which were already way above anything else on offer back home. For example, the inaugural Indianapolis 500 International Sweepstake, as it was billed, posted a total purse of $27,500. Eventual winner Ray Harroun took home a lion's share of $10,000, plus an extra $4250 in contingency money. The following year, Joe Dawson earned almost double that – and remember this was in an era when the best a factory worker could expect to earn in a year was around $650. Not bad loot, thank you very much.

The success of Indianapolis and the high-speed board tracks led to a major boom through the next decade. The Roaring Twenties were in full swing. As prize money increased, so the cars and engines became more sophisticated; and the entire scenario seemed set to benefit from a rationalized set of regulations which ensured cars could race on either side of 'The Pond'.

In 1921, when, controversially, the American 3.0-litre regulations were adopted for the Automobile Club de France's annual 'Grand Prix', which was to be held that year on a 10.75-mile road course at Le Mans, the German-born Duesenberg brothers, Fred and Augie, boldly decided to see if they could out-European the Europeans. They figured that if the Europeans could vanquish the best of the Americans, as they had in the early years at Indy, then they should try to return the favour.

The Duesenbergs' radical straight-eight cylinder engines had proved their performance back home, winning most of the races – but not Indianapolis – in 1920. Now they were to take on the all-conquering Ballots and Talbots on their home turf, in the first Grand Prix to be held in the post-war era. And the Americans, with a four-car team managed by veteran driver George Robertson, were determined to succeed.

Irish-American Jimmy Murphy emerged victorious from an incredibly dramatic race, despite the fact his 'Duesie' had a leaking fuel tank, a holed radiator and a burst tyre! It was a sensational success, one in the eye for the French. (It would also remain, incidentally, as the first and only Grand Prix win for an American car and an American driver until Dan Gurney's Eagle flew to victory in the 1967 Belgian Grand Prix at Spa.)

The Duesenberg team returned home in triumph and its cars continued in the same winning vein. Curiously, though, the trans-Atlantic interaction didn't continue to develop as expected. The cars were similar enough, but in Europe the emphasis was still very much on road racing – as, of course, it remains today – whereas the Americans concentrated almost exclusively on the ovals. The two disciplines required entirely different skills, and, speaking from my own experience at Indy this year, they still do.

Consequently, and as the sport in America increased in popularity, so the European influence began to wane. Another intuitive engineer, Harry Miller, soon augmented the work of the Duesenbergs by firmly establishing the fact that American technology was at least a match for anything the Europeans could produce. In 1922, Murphy achieved his goal of a victory at Indianapolis, using a Miller-engined Duesenberg. Murphy also became the first driver to win the race after starting from pole position.

Miller was responsible for several interesting innovations, including the first use of aluminium pistons and engine blocks. Combining his own talents with those of draftsman Leo Goossen and machinist Fred Offenhauser, he soon became the dominant supplier both of cars and engines. The equipment was expensive by the standards of the time, but it was good. It was the best. It was the latter-day equivalent of the Williams-Renault, if you like. Basically, if you wanted to be competitive in the late '20s, you needed a Miller. Or to pinch the slogan from a modern-day beer advertisement, it was Miller Time! Tommy Milton continued the Miller theme when he became the first two-time Indy 500 winner in 1923, repeating his success of two years earlier.

Peter De Paolo was also a well-known name in those early days, winning the race and the championship in 1925. His equally famous uncle, Ralph De Palma, also won a pair of AAA National Championships (1912 and 1914) and the Indianapolis 500 (1915). De Paolo earned a majestic $90,000 for his efforts.

Another star from this exciting era was Frank Lockhart, who burst onto the scene in 1926. I think it's fair to say he was regarded in much the same way as we have hailed Gilles Villeneuve or Ayrton Senna or Michael Schumacher as potential giants of our sport in more recent years.

The 23-year-old Lockhart, a frequent dirt-track winner in his native California, travelled to Indianapolis, the 'Mecca' of racing, with the same hopes and dreams as countless others. He was invited to take a few laps during practice and was immediately impressive, displaying a youthful bravado and skill that stood out from the crowd. Despite the fact he had never raced on a paved track before, Lockhart was pencilled in as a potential relief driver should one be needed. Then, a few days before the race, a 'flu-ridden Peter Kreis realized he wasn't going to be fit enough to drive. He offered the car, a Miller of course, to Lockhart. It was an inspired move, and an opportunity the youngster grabbed eagerly. Inside sixty laps he had moved up into the lead. A dozen laps later, the race was halted due to a persistent drizzle. Undeterred, Lockhart carried on at the re-start from where he left off, and when the rain returned after 160 laps, 400 miles, he was still in front – more than two laps ahead of the nearest

The exquisite Miller 91 was a dominant force in the 1500cc era. In 1926, Frank Lockhart scorched to victory in his very first Indianapolis 500 start.

opposition. He had scored a famous victory.

Lockhart, at the behest of Harry Miller, completed the season and earned enough points to finish second in the AAA National Championship standings. Their partnership was spectacular; the brilliant young driver and the innovative engineer. But Lockhart also had his heart set on breaking the World Land Speed Record. He came close with the streamlined Stutz 'Black Hawk', only to be killed during an attempt at Daytona Beach, Florida, when a burst tyre sent him somersaulting down the sand.

There were other legendary names from those exciting inter-war years. Among them was Captain Eddie Rickenbacker. He, like many others, became enraptured by motor sport. He competed with some success in the early 1900s but earned far greater recognition as a fighter ace in World War One with 26 confirmed 'kills' to his credit. Rickenbacker continued his links with aviation by founding Eastern Air Lines. He maintained his motor racing ties by taking over Indianapolis in 1927.

That same year saw Louie Meyer, another of the legendary names in Indy Car racing, make the switch from mechanic to driver. Meyer, whose father had been one of the racing pioneers, was standing in the pits when Wilbur Shaw came in and needed a relief driver. It was a question of being in the right place at the right time. Meyer drove for 41 laps, whereupon Shaw resumed at the wheel and finished fourth.

Relief drivers were a common phenomenon in those days, and in fact they continued to be so right through into the 1950s. The races were gruelling affairs, and if the driver felt tired, or otherwise below par, he would think nothing of diving into the pits and finding a suitable replacement either to take over for a few laps or even, more rarely, to finish the race.

Such was the manner in which Meyer's career as a driver was born. It turned out to be some career, too. The following year, at the wheel of a Miller (what else?), Meyer started 13th but it certainly wasn't unlucky as he sped home to victory in what was effectively his first major race. He went on to win the championship as well that year. Meyer repeated as AAA National Champion in 1929, the first man ever to win back-to-back titles. He would have won Indianapolis again, too, but for a time-consuming pit stop a little before three-quarters distance.

Meyer won Indy twice more. Both victories had a historical significance. In 1933, dehydrated as a result of his exertions during the race, which lasted almost five hours, he asked for – and quickly received – a drink of milk in Victory Lane. Three years later his spoils of victory included the magnificent new sterling silver Borg–Warner Trophy as well as the keys to the pace car: a brand new Packard. Since then, the trophy, the bottle of milk and the pace car have developed into traditions, symbols of victory at Indy which have continued to this day – although Emerson Fittipaldi was roundly criticized this year when he eschewed the traditional 'pinta' in Victory Lane in favour of a bottle of his Brazilian-produced and marketed orange juice. In fact, the next weekend, when we raced in Milwaukee, Emerson was booed when he was introduced to the crowd during the traditional hoopla prior to the race. The state of Wisconsin, you see, is the primary milk producer in the United States. Emerson was not a popular figure at all.

But those inter-war years represented lean times for Indianapolis-type

Above The prodigiously talented Frank Lockhart lost his life in the ill-fated Stutz 'Black Hawk' which featured a pair of eight-cylinder Miller engines mounted on a common crankcase.

Right The Speedway Hall of Fame Museum contains more than 30 Indy 500-winning cars as well as the Lotus 29 with which Jimmy Clark finished second in the '500' in 1962.

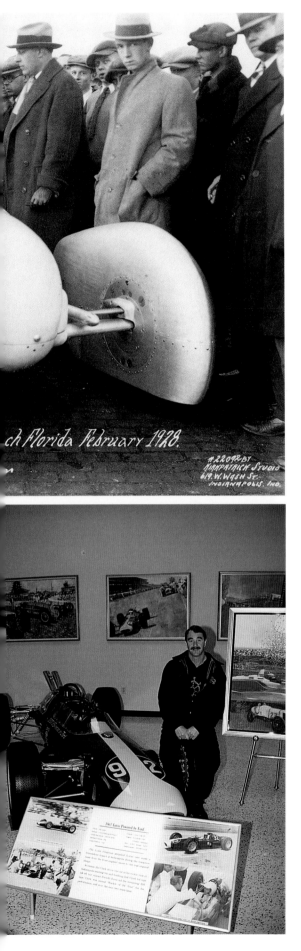

ch Florida February 1928.

#22098 BY
KIRKPATRICK STUDIO
619 W. WASH ST.
INDIANAPOLIS, IND.

racing. The American economy had hit rock bottom, and motor racing did not escape the ravages of The Great Depression.

Harry Miller was one of myriad business casualties. When there was no longer a queue to buy his latest and greatest and hang the expense, even his imaginative talent fell by the wayside.

In 1933, Fred Offenhauser came to the rescue by taking over the manufacturing of Miller-designed engines. Under austere circumstances he managed to keep things afloat.

Leo Goossen remained an integral part of the company, to be joined by another gifted Californian engineer named Art Sparks. The newly badged Offenhauser engines continued on their winning way. In fact, Offenhauser, Goossen, Sparks and Meyer, who in partnership with Dale Drake took over the company again in 1946, continued to provide a variety of powerplants which were to dominate the sport for the next forty years, until the advent of the Formula 1-derived Ford/Cosworth DFX.

The sport continued even in the midst of the Depression, helped by the fact the old rag, tag and bobtail set of technical regulations had been replaced by a formula which placed a greater emphasis on production-based machinery. Technical innovations began to creep in again, with our old pal Harry Miller springing up once more, this time in partnership with famed promoter Preston Tucker and the Ford Motor Company to produce the startling Miller-Fords which first appeared in 1935. Among the cars' many features were front-wheel drive, fully independent suspension and fared-in axles to promote a streamlined shape.

The cars looked great, but there was barely enough time to build them, let alone develop them. Only four of the ten cars qualified and all fell out of the race due to a steering problem. They also cost a lot more money than had been envisaged initially. The project was an expensive and dismal failure.

Undaunted, two years later the Gulf Oil Company commissioned Miller to develop a car with only one goal in mind: victory at Indianapolis. The car was a work of art. It mirrored the German-developed Auto-Unions in featuring a mid-engine layout, streamlined bodywork and inboard-mounted dampers. We take those characteristics for granted nowadays of course, but back then they were virtually unheard-of. But wait, there was more. The supercharged six-cylinder drove all four wheels, and through his imaginative design Miller achieved an almost perfect 50–50 weight distribution.

The cars, however, because of their complexity, were late in being constructed. And incredibly expensive. And dangerous. Three of the four cars built were destroyed by fire. The other one is now housed safely in the amazing Indianapolis Motor Speedway Museum, which ranks alongside Tom Wheatcroft's Donington Park, as an evocative reminder of times past.

The disastrous Gulf-Millers nevertheless provided an example of how sponsorship had become prevalent in America. They also served as evidence that the advances in racing-car design being made in Europe had not gone unnoticed.

This renewed interaction between engineers separated by the Atlantic Ocean continued to develop when a group of enthusiasts on the East Coast joined together in 1936 to resurrect the Vanderbilt Cup on Long Island, New York. Their intention, with the AAA Championship reduced to a

bare minimum of races by the ravages of the Depression, was to attract international entries and perhaps inject some fresh enthusiasm in the sport.

They succeeded. There weren't many takers in the first year but Tazio Nuvolari, acknowledged as one of the greatest racers of all time, swept the field for Alfa Romeo. The following year the mighty German teams of Auto-Union and Mercedes joined in. They proved even more dominant, with the equally talented Bernd Rosemeyer winning for Auto-Union. It was the first-ever Championship success for a rear-engined car and, incredibly, would remain so for a further 26 years! Rex Mays, one of the brightest of the American stars, finished a game third in a year-old Alfa Romeo.

In 1937, the regulations at Indianapolis were changed to once more allow the use of superchargers, while at the same time mandating the use of pump fuel (or gasoline as it's universally known in America) instead of an unholy brew which included all sorts of wonderful concoctions and had become known as 'dope'.

I'm sure many of the teams looked upon the changes with open disdain, just as did the Formula 1 teams last year when the 'rocket fuel' brews were outlawed. It didn't matter. Gas was in, dope was out.

A year later, the transition from the so-called 'Junk Formula' was completed by simple adoption of the new regulations specified in Europe by the International Sporting Commission (CSI) of the French-based governing body, the Association Internationale de l'Automobile Clubs Reconnus (AIACR). Curiously, the motorsports' world had turned full circle. In 1920, the French authorities had based the new Grand Prix rules

Tazio Nuvolari poses for a picture in Louis Meyer's Bowes Seal Fast Special. Nuvolari did win a race on Long Island for Maserati in 1936 but never actually drove at The Speedway.

on those used in America. Now it was the other way around.

Anxious to curb the ever-increasing power output of the monstrous and hugely expensive Auto-Unions and Mercedes, which by then were producing upwards of 600 bhp, the CSI scrapped the old 750 kilogram (1653 lb) formula in favour of one permitting a maximum engine size of 4.5 litres, or 3.0 litres supercharged. It was the first attempt to equalize the performance of supercharged and non-supercharged cars. In addition there was a sliding scale of minimum weight versus engine displacement. Riding mechanics were out too. From now on the purest of racing cars would be single-seat (Monoposto) only.

The new rules were unsuccessful as an attempt to curb the dominance of the German teams. Adolf Hitler's cohorts simply provided the necessary funding for new designs. But the changes did bring about the return of dope to Indianapolis, since special fuels were still permitted by the CSI. They also served to show how much the Europeans had gained over the Americans, a fact confirmed by the home side's crushing defeats in the Vanderbilt Cup events. Even though money remained scarce in America, some teams began shopping around. None of the dominant German cars were available at the time, but year-old Alfas and Maseratis could be bought at reasonable cost.

Both Mays (Alfa) and Mauri Rose (Maserati) ran well enough at Indy in '38, although the cars were clearly lacking in the reliability department. The following year Wilbur Shaw triumphed in a very special Maserati 8CLT, modified and updated to cope with the abnormal stresses involved at Indianapolis. The same combination won again the following year, and Shaw was en route to become the first man to win the race in three consecutive years until a wheel failure pitched him out of the lead in 1941.

The foreign cars, however, were expensive to run, especially when compared to the home-built chassis and 'Offy' engines which still comprised the bulk of the field. Shaw's team, bankrolled by Chicago industrialist Mike Boyle, was a league apart.

In 1940 and '41, only three races, including Indy, were held as part of the AAA Championship. The others were on one-mile dirt ovals, as far removed from Indianapolis in terms of characteristics as they could possibly be. The American cars were far superior under those circumstances, as they were on the bread-and-butter short ovals which continued to provide entertainment for fans around the country. In the Championship events, Mays took his all-American Stevens-Winfield to victory both at Springfield, Illinois, and Syracuse, New York, in 1940 as well as at Milwaukee, Wisconsin, and Syracuse again the following year to claim a pair of AAA titles.

By this time, of course, World War II had taken a firm grip. There was no escape, even for racing. It wasn't until the end of hostilities in 1945 that the sport began to evolve once more. The following May, the Indianapolis Motor Speedway hosted the first post-war AAA event. Whereas in Europe a brand-new formula had been introduced, the promoters in North America wisely decided to remain largely with what they had, since there were plenty of cars which complied with the pre-war regulations. The only significant change was a relaxation of the previous minimum weight limit.

The result was a boom in interest. The war itself had fostered many technological advances, especially in the aircraft industry, and it wasn't long before many of the benefits were being applied to motor racing. Features such as tubular spaceframes, cast magnesium wheels and disc brakes had proven their worth in combat and soon became commonplace on the race track.

Initially, however, the older cars triumphed, more the result of consistency than pace. American-built cars led the way, although Maserati entered a factory team at Indy in 1946, with Italian Grand Prix star Luigi Villoresi finishing seventh. The same car with which Wilbur Shaw had dominated the pre-war proceedings placed third, this time in the capable hands of Ted Horn, who reverted to a more conventional Offy-powered car for the other races and went on to claim a hat-trick of AAA titles.

One of the superb Mercedes W154 Grand Prix cars also appeared a couple of times at Indy. The only problem was that it was running in private hands. The gorgeous supercharged V12-powered machine was certainly fast enough – Duke Nalon was second quickest in 1947, although he started way back on row six as a second-day qualifier – but it failed to possess the necessary reliability for 500 miles.

The relatively affluent post-war era also brought forth some incredible designs. Among them was the 1946 Fageol Twin Coach Special, featuring not one but two Offenhauser midget engines, one in front of the driver, the other behind, which drove through a pair of specially adapted front-wheel drive transmissions as used on the unsuccessful Miller-Fords. Hey presto: four-wheel drive! Except the two engines were connected only by a common throttle linkage; they drove each end of the car independently. The car was heavy but it was quick, and Paul Russo qualified impressively in the middle of the front row.

Other interesting concepts included the two-cylinder front-wheel drive Suttle Steamer which was billed as comprising only sixteen moving parts. Not surprisingly perhaps, the car was never seen. But the Pat Clancy Special was. Six wheels and all. The brainchild of a Memphis, Tennessee-based trucking company owner, the car looked conventional enough from the cockpit forward, powered by a regular front-mounted Meyer-Drake Offy engine. But behind were a pair of Midget-type axles, both of which were driven. The Pat Clancy Special demonstrated excellent traction capabilities and good handling, as per its design rationale. It finished 12th at Indy in 1948 and a best of fourth the following season on the Milwaukee Mile.

Some people may scoff at the idea now, but the same concept was tried in Formula 1 many years later. March concocted its novel '2–4–0' design in 1976, while six years later even Williams produced a six-wheel derivative of the successful FW08. Neither car raced.

And what about a diesel engine? The Cummins Engine Company entered several cars at Indianapolis, with the most ambitious effort in 1952 featuring a turbocharged 6.6-litre truck engine fitted to a sleek low-line chassis specially designed by Frank Kurtis. Freddie Agabashian qualified the diesel on the pole at an impressive 138.01 mph.

Then there were the nerve-tingling Novis, the name derived from the small Michigan town in which originator Lew Welch lived, at the sixth exit, No. VI, on the old Detroit–Lansing toll road. The Novis were to American audiences what the BRMs were to British enthusiasts in the 1950s and

'60s. The centrifugally supercharged 3-litre V8 engines were penned by the prolific Leo Goossen to a concept dreamed up by Welch and Bud Winfield. And they sounded, to use the American vernacular, awesome.

Development of the pre-war motor continued right through until 1965, but its speed was tempered by a voracious fuel consumption. The cars consequently needed to carry a larger fuel cell, so they were heavy and hard on tyres. Duke Nalon claimed a couple of poles for the Novi marque, but his and Novi's best-ever finish was third in 1948.

The front-wheel drive Blue Crown Spark Plug Specials were markedly more successful, finishing one-two in both 1947 and '48.

The Indianapolis creations aside, AAA National Championship races were dominated by traditional sit-up-and-beg 'dirt cars' and Offy (Meyer-Drake) four-cylinder engines. Indeed after Louis Unser, driving a pre-war Maserati, won the 1947 Pikes Peak Hillclimb, which counted back then as a championship event, Offy-powered cars won an incredible 99 races in a row. The string was broken only in 1955, again at Pikes Peak, when Bob Finney's Lincoln slithered its way to the top, whereupon the Offy engines embarked on another long streak. This time it stretched 98 races before Scotland's Jimmy Clark sped to victory in a Ford-powered Lotus at Milwaukee in 1963.

The ubiquitous Offenhausers were as dominant as the Ford/Cosworth DFV was to become in Formula 1 during the 1970s and the subsequent DFX derivative was to the Indy Car scene in the late 1970s and '80s. The Offy was relatively simple, reliable and inexpensive, which meant it could be plugged in to a wide variety of different chassis – again, in just the same way as the DFV spawned the 'kit-car' era in Grand Prix racing.

Jimmy Clark was a brilliant – and brave – champion. His 1963 Lotus offered minimal protection for the driver.

Gradually, though, the old ladder-frame chassis were replaced by tubular spaceframe designs, and the versatile cars which had proven equally competitive on dirt ovals, the few paved circuits as well as Indianapolis were eclipsed by more up-to-date technology. The sport became much more specialized. A fresh nomenclature followed. Cars built specifically for the Indy 500 had become known as Speedway cars, while those used primarily on shorter paved ovals, which became more prevalent through the 1950s and '60s, attracted the moniker Champ cars, referring to the increasingly popular National Championship. And those used for the rough-and-tumble short tracks earned the name Sprint cars.

Frank Kurtis's Cummins Diesel Speedway car of 1952 was a precursor of things to come. The next year he adopted similar principles to a conventional Offy engine, which was modified to lie on its side and mated to an offset drive-train. The result was a lower centre of gravity and a distinct weight bias to the left-hand side, which was perfect for the left-handed ovals. At a stroke, handling characteristics and perhaps even more significantly tyre wear had been dramatically improved.

The low-line 'Roadsters' immediately dominated the scene as convincingly as had Miller's cars in the 1920s. They came in various different guises, the most successful of them subsequently devised by legendary chief mechanic A. J. Watson, and remained in control for the next ten years – until the next major 'revolution' hit the Indy Car circuit.

In the meantime, the face of motor racing worldwide had been changed by the events of a tragic three-week period in May and June of 1955. First, just a few days after surviving an incident in which his Lancia plunged into the harbour during the Monaco Grand Prix, two-time World Drivers' Champion Alberto Ascari lost his life while testing a Ferrari sports car at

High up on the banking at Monza in 1958, the incomparable Stirling Moss and his specially built Maserati lead defending AAA National Champion and Indianapolis 500 winner Jimmy Bryan, driving the same Salih-Offy driven to victory at Indy in 1957 by Sam Hanks, and Luigi Musso's hybrid Ferrari.

Monza. Four days later, popular Bill Vukovich was killed at Indianapolis while seemingly cruising towards what would have been his third straight 500-mile victory.

Then came Le Mans. More than 80 spectators perished and scores more were injured when a Mercedes-Benz 300SLR driven by Pierre 'Levegh' somersaulted into a crowded public enclosure directly in front of the pits. It was a ghastly scene.

The accidents had far-reaching consequences. Motor racing was banned in several countries, while the American Automobile Association concluded it could no longer conscience the sanctioning of motorsports. It was bad for the image.

Enter the United States Auto Club.

Founded by Anton 'Tony' Hulman Jr., who also had been largely responsible for resurrecting the Indianapolis Motor Speedway following the ravages of neglect during World War II, USAC was just what American motor sports needed: a professional sanctioning body. Former driver Duane Carter became the first Director of Competition, and the organization was able to orchestrate a smooth transition from the AAA days with no adverse effects on the thriving sport.

USAC also took over management of Sprint car and Midget races, as well as stock car events and even some sports car road racing. For the first time, American racing had a properly structured 'ladder of opportunity', with, as ever, the Indianapolis 500 and the National Championship providing the primary focus.

A slight downsizing of the engines was decreed soon after USAC took control of the series, although the smaller displacement had virtually no effect on speeds, which continued to creep upwards. In 1958, one year after the new rule took effect, Dick Rathmann qualified his Watson roadster on pole at Indy with a new track record of 145.974 mph.

Throughout the 1950s there was precious little interaction between Europe and America, despite the fact Indianapolis was included as a round of the World Drivers' Championship for most of the decade. The only real exceptions were a token entry at Indy by Ferrari in 1952 and a couple of curious events on the incredibly bumpy and horribly dangerous Autodromo di Monza oval in 1957 and '58. I tell you what, I'm glad I wasn't old enough to race in those days!

Brooklands had long since fallen by the wayside, and for some reason the authorities in Monza decided it would be a good idea to build a super-speedway oval, *à la Indianapolis*. The huge high-banked edifice was completed in 1955, shortly after the Le Mans catastrophe. Apart from being used in conjunction with the existing road course for the Italian Grand Prix, it lay dormant for two years before an agreement was reached for ten American cars and stars to travel east and take on the cream of the European competition. Unfortunately, the only European takers for 'The Race of Two Worlds' were a trio of Ecurie Ecosse D-Type Jaguars, the Scottish team 'fresh' from its glorious success at Le Mans the previous weekend, and a motley collection of privateers.

The event was largely a dud, although Tony Bettenhausen (father of the Tony B. who now enters Stefan Johansson in the Indy Car series) did raise some eyebrows by establishing a new closed course record at over 176 mph in the ear-splitting Novi. As ever, the car didn't last. Defending USAC champion Jimmy Bryan dominated the three-heat affair in an Eddie Kuzma-built roadster.

The following year's repeat performance did show signs of improvement, with a cobbled-up works-entered V12 Ferrari qualifying on pole in the hands of the extraordinarily brave Luigi Musso, but after that the concept was quietly forgotten.

The next European challenge to the Americans was altogether more serious. Ever since the inauguration of the World Drivers' Championship in 1950, the regulations for Indianapolis-type racing and Formula 1 had been significantly different; cross-pollination was rare. And when, for 1961, the Federation Internationale de l'Automobile (FIA) decided that Formula 1 cars needed to be slowed drastically, hence a new 1.5-litre formula in place of the old 2.5-litre category, the two worlds seemed farther apart than ever.

The British Formula 1 teams lobbied long and hard against the new rules, but to no avail. Eventually, when the 1961 season started, they were left struggling to catch up with the gorgeous V6-powered 'Shark Nose' Ferrari Dino 156s, with which Phil Hill went on to become America's first-ever Formula 1 World Champion. But it wasn't long before the Brits caught up again.

They had ruled the roost in previous years, led by the trend-setting rear-engined Cooper-Climaxes which had been developed from a succession of far less powerful but incredibly effective rear-engined 500cc formula cars. Colin Chapman followed the fashion with his Lotus 18. By 1961 it was apparent that having the engine mounted behind the driver was the way to go forward.

Two years earlier, America had hosted two rounds of the World Championship, with Indianapolis joined on the calendar by an altogether more suitable event for Formula 1 machinery on the Sebring airfield course in Florida. USAC star Rodger Ward was among the crowd that weekend. He was immediately impressed by the handling capabilities of the nimble little Formula 1 cars. Ward soon started probing John Cooper about the prospects of taking one of his cars to Indianapolis for a trial run.

In typical Cooper fashion, a full year passed before the test took place. Finally, on the way back from the final race of the Formula 1 season, which in 1960 was at Riverside, California, one of the cars was dispatched to Indiana along with works driver Jack Brabham. The diminutive Cooper was fast from the outset. Brabham quickly sailed through his mandatory rookie orientation programme and within a couple of days had recorded a best lap at 144.834 mph. It would have been 11th fastest among that year's 33-car field. And this was with a bog-standard Formula 1 car and a regular 2.5-litre engine which produced perhaps 230 bhp. The 4.2-litre Offys, by contrast, punched out close to twice that much.

Where the Cooper scored, of course, was in the handling department; it was comparatively slow on the straights – sorry, straightaways, as I'm constantly being reminded they're called in America – but significantly swifter through the corners.

Cooper and Brabham returned to England consumed with the prospect of victory at Indianapolis. They knew full well the lucre that could be gained.

JACK BRABHAM · 1961 · INDIANAPOLIS MOTOR SPEEDWAY

USAC waived the regulation mandating a minimum eight-foot wheelbase to allow Jack Brabham's trend-setting Cooper Climax to compete in 1961.

The 1960 winner, Jim Rathmann, had pocketed a staggering $110,000 for his efforts.

There was more good news, too, since wealthy Jim Kimberly, an amateur sports car racer who was also head of the Kleenex clan, had agreed to sponsor an all-expenses-paid Cooper effort at Indy in 1961. A good deal of work was put into the project. The Climax engine was enlarged to 2.7 litres and tilted in the specially built chassis to aid weight distribution. Brabham qualified comfortably enough, 13th, and the tiny, incongruous-looking Cooper flitted in and out among the rumbling roadsters to earn a respectable ninth-place finish despite making three longer-than-scheduled pit stops.

It was the beginning of the end for the American roadsters. The following year California Hot Rod king Mickey Thompson produced a more advanced clone of the Cooper, powered by a 4.2-litre stock-block Buick V8. Fellow Californian Dan Gurney, who for a few years had been impressing the Europeans with his prowess in Grand Prix cars, qualified a strong eighth. But the astute Gurney had already realized there was a bunch of people who could do an even better job in designing a rear-engined Indianapolis car.

37

Lotus boss Colin Chapman, for one. Gurney was driving for Porsche in Formula 1 that season, and Chapman's wonderful 'bathtub' monocoque chassis Lotus 25 was clearly the class of the field. Jimmy Clark qualified on pole for six of the season's nine races. Only mechanical frailty prevented the great Scot from claiming his first World Championship.

Right after the 25's debut at Zandvoort in the 1962 Dutch Grand Prix, lured by a free airline ticket, Colin travelled to Indianapolis to watch Gurney and the others in action.

Coincidentally, the Ford Motor Company, which had eschewed an involvement at Indianapolis ever since the Miller-Ford fiasco in 1935, was considering a change of heart. Ford soon decided to side with Lotus instead of a potential deal with Watson, whose front-engined cars had won four years' running at Indy. So Chapman went to work. The result, penned by Len Terry from a brief supplied by Chapman, was the Lotus 29, a much stronger version of the 25. It was powered by a potent 4.2-litre Ford V8 derived from the Fairlane pushrod engine but now featuring alloy crankcase, block and cylinder heads.

Clark and Gurney were to drive the exciting new cars, both fitted with the lightweight Fords which were on a par power-wise with all the other American engines.

In the meantime USAC regular Lloyd Ruby shook the establishment by leading for 40 laps of the 1963 USAC season opener at Trenton, New Jersey, in an aging Formula 1 Lotus-Climax 18. The writing was on the wall.

At Indianapolis, however, former Sprint and Midget star Parnelli Jones scored a controversial victory in his Watson roadster despite trailing a plume of smoke which nine times out of 10 would have earned him a black flag and necessitated a pit stop to check for leaks. Clark, Chapman and Lotus had to settle for second (with Gurney seventh); but that result served only to strengthen their resolve.

Later in the season, after Clark had all but clinched his first Formula 1 crown, he and the Lotus-Ford dominated proceedings at Milwaukee, qualifying on pole at a new lap record of 109.303 mph (the old mark, incidentally, stood to Don Branson at 105.603 mph). Clark lapped all but A. J. Foyt in second place, again at a record pace. It was much the same story at Trenton. Clark again annihilated the qualifying record, only to retire, as did Gurney, with engine problems.

In '64, Clark qualified easily on the pole at Indy, his slightly revised Lotus 34 fitted with the latest four-cam Ford V8. Clark bettered the track record by a startling 7.675 mph, leaving the new standard at 158.828 mph. It was the largest single increase in lap speeds since Georges Boillot's equally advanced Peugeot smashed the previous record by no less than 11.41 mph in 1914.

Talented youngster Bobby Marshman sat alongside Clark on the front row in a modified 29. The two Lotuses were significantly faster than anything else. This time, in a race marred by the deaths of Eddie Sachs and Dave MacDonald in a horrible fiery crash, both cars fell out early; but it was only a matter of time. Clark was unbeatable with his new Lotus 38 in 1965, gaining revenge over Parnelli Jones, who finished second in an earlier Lotus 34.

Clark tested a Formula 1 Lotus 25 for Colin Chapman at Indianapolis directly after the 1962 United States Grand Prix at Watkins Glen. A promising run helped to clinch the deal with Ford for the following season.

Dan Gurney, who was instrumental in persuading Chapman to enter Indy, was running in third place with the team's prototype Lotus 29 until having to make an extra pit stop to tighten the rear wheel nuts.

By now the vast majority of the field was equipped with rear-engined cars. And Fords were the engine of choice.

The rapid increase in performance from the lightweight cars fostered direct competition between tyre manufacturers for the first time in many years. Dunlops were used by the Lotus team in 1964 (although in 1965 they switched back to the previously ubiquitous Firestones), while Goodyear also joined the fray, winning for the first time in the modern era in 1967. It was Firestone's first defeat since 1919.

The rivalry between Firestone and Goodyear continued for another seven years, escalating into what amounted to a full-scale war between the two Akron, Ohio-based giants until Firestone finally withdrew amid much acrimony in 1974. The result of the rivalry, once again, was a steady increase in cornering speeds.

The tyre companies also contributed greatly to the sport through the introduction of foam-filled rubber-bladder fuel cells which were developed from military helicopters. The bladders were made mandatory following the Sachs/MacDonald inferno, as was the use of methanol fuel, far less volatile than regular gasoline. Those two innovations improved safety aspects dramatically. USAC also introduced a minimum weight limit for the first time since before the war. That, too, helped to eliminate some of the dangerous lightweight specials which appeared from time to time.

The sport continued to grow through the 1960s. Paved ovals had by now become the backbone of the series, with only a handful of dirt venues remaining. The shift towards mid-engined cars also led USAC to experiment with a few road course races, starting with Indianapolis Raceway Park in 1965. It represented the National Championship's first visit to a road course since the Vanderbilt Cup race on Long Island in 1937. And who should emerge victorious but my very own teammate this year, Mario Andretti. I was thirteen at the time, and wondering how I was going to fare in my next go-kart race. It seems like a long time ago!

The new breed of Indy cars clearly were suited to those type of tracks, and more promoters soon jumped on the bandwagon. Mosport Park and St Jovite, both in Canada, were added to the list in 1967, along with Riverside, home of the 1960 United States Grand Prix.

Andretti, Gurney and the Unser brothers, Bobby and Al (nephews of nine-time Pikes Peak winner Louis Unser), won the first sixteen road course races between them, save for one win by Foyt at Castle Rock, Colorado, in 1968. That same year, in fact, there were no less than nine road course events, three of which featured two-part races. The Pikes Peak Hillclimb also counted among the record total of twenty-eight races, ensuring the USAC National Championship was a true test of versatility. And stamina. At the end of the year, Bobby Unser edged Andretti to the title by a mere 11 points, 4330 to 4319. Al Unser followed in third place.

These three, along with the incomparable Foyt, took control of the sport between 1963 and 1971. They won a total of 100 (out of 162) races in that nine-year-span and indeed continued to be major forces right through into the 1980s. Foyt, especially, was the epitome of the American racer. The tough-as-nails Texan won 10 out of the 13 races in 1964, dominating in a manner never seen before or since. He amassed an unmatched seven National Championships, four Indy 500s and no fewer than 67 Indy Car

Mario Andretti in his younger days, celebrating victory on the Indianapolis Raceway Park road course in 1966 with one of Indy car racing's legendary chief mechanics, Clint Brawner.

wins in a career that ended only this May when, at the age of 58, Foyt surprised just about everyone by suddenly announcing his retirement.

While Foyt and his on-track rivals maintained a form of stability in the sport, technological advances continued apace. The evergreen Goossen and Drake refused to be downhearted by the mid-'60s dominance of the quad-cam Ford, not even when long-time associate Louie Meyer jumped ship. Instead they ploughed on with development of the venerable Offy engine. This time, following an extensive redesign which included the addition of a turbocharger, the four-cylinder dinosaur, downsized to 2.7 litres, took on a new lease of life. The engine which first started to win races in the '30s was competitive once more.

Stock-blocks also were lured back into the fold as part of a conscious attempt by USAC to restrict costs and at the same time entice more automobile manufacturers into the sport. The ploy didn't really work, despite raising the maximum size of the production-based engines to 5.0 litres and then, in 1969, to 5.25 litres. Only Dan Gurney's V8 was truly competitive, based initially on a Ford block with cylinder heads provided by British engineering genius Harry Weslake.

Since 1971, every Indy Car race bar one has been won by a turbocharged engine. The only exception was a 150-mile race at Milwaukee in 1981, when Mike Mosley scored an upset victory with one of Gurney's Eagle-Chevrolets.

One other interesting form of motivation, a jet turbine, was tried in the '60s, with some success. The flamboyant Andy Granatelli, boss of the STP Additives division of the Studebaker Corporation, having tried and failed to make the Novi project a winner, instead located a Pratt & Whitney jet helicopter engine. For the 1967 Indianapolis 500, this potent piece was slotted into a purpose-built chassis commissioned from yet another British engineer, Ken Wallis. Our famous friend Parnelli Jones was signed to drive the car, and after qualifying comfortably on the second row, the canny Jones waited until raceday to unleash the all-wheel drive car's full potential. It was sensational. Jones quickly carved his way to the front and was seemingly on his way to Victory Lane until a minor failure in the transmission manifested itself with only three laps remaining. It was another case of 'so near and yet so far' at Indianapolis.

The story in 1968 was depressingly similar for Granatelli. This time he had ordered brand-new cars from Lotus. The Maurice Phillippe-designed Type 56 was the pace-setter. Joe Leonard earned the pole at a new record 171.559 mph. Teammate Graham Hill was just a tad slower. A third car for Art Pollard also was safely in the field. Once again none made it to the finish, Pollard and Leonard retiring almost within sight of each other with less than a dozen laps remaining.

A development of those same cars was used to good effect for a while in Formula 1, but they were never again competitive in Indy Car racing due to a clamp down on the rules by the decidedly itchy USAC board.

The early 1970s brought several significant changes to the USAC series. In 1970, after Indianapolis boasted its first $1 million purse fund, a second 500-mile race was added to the schedule at the magnificent new Ontario Motor Speedway in Southern California. It was a virtual copy of Indianapolis, but its new smooth track ensured it was significantly faster. That same year the high-banked 2-mile Michigan International Speedway was added as a regular fixture, initially as a 200-mile race, while in 1971 the 2.5-mile tri-oval (three-cornered) Pocono International Raceway also hosted its first 500-mile race.

At the same time, USAC had been collaborating with the Sports Car Club of America (SCCA) in sanctioning events for the thriving Formula 5000 category. Now it was decided that Formula 5000 would concentrate on road courses, leaving the Indy cars to race on ovals. So for 1971, reflecting also an increased focus on longer races on faster tracks, the series was run for the first time on a solitary diet of paved ovals, ranging from the one-mile tracks at Milwaukee and Phoenix, Arizona, through to the 2.5-mile super-speedways at Indy, Pocono and Ontario. It was the first time the 'traditional' dirt ovals had been dropped from the schedule, reaffirming the increasing specialization of the Speedway cars. Al Unser, incidentally, had the honour of winning the last loose-surface National Championship race, at Sacramento, California, in 1970, after which the dirt tracks were left to host their own USAC Silver Crown Championship for the old-style Champ cars.

This new accent for the premier series led to the teams focusing their

Parnelli Jones and 'Silent Sam', as he called the car—or the 'Whooshmobile' as it was dubbed by the press—almost won at Indianapolis in 1967.

Taking the theme of jet turbines a step further, Joe Leonard and Graham Hill (*right*) blitzed the field in qualifying for the 1968 Indianapolis 500, although neither Lotus finished.

attention almost entirely on ways of increasing two basic features: aero-dynamic efficiency and reliable horsepower. The shape of the cars was to be changed forever.

Inverted aerofoils, or 'wings' as they became known, had become preva-lent in Formula 1 in 1968 as a means of providing downforce, and therefore grip, through the corners. Indy car designers had always assumed straight-line speed to be of paramount importance, but as soon as they realized the key to straight-line speed was provided by a fast exit to the corners, wings began to sprout at Indianapolis, too. Before long they were an inherent feature of any Indy car design, although USAC rules at first called for all aerodynamic devices to be an integral part of the bodywork.

The wings were used to augment the sleek 'wedge-shape' design concept, pioneered by the Lotus turbine car and perpetuated by Chapman's World Championship-winning Lotus 72 in 1970. Side-mounted radiators also were featured on the trend-setting type 72, and first appeared on the Indy Car scene the following year with Gordon Coppuck's McLaren M16.

The new breed was partly responsible for an incredible escalation of speed at Indianapolis. In 1970, winner Al Unser qualified his George Bignotti-built Colt, which was derived from the previous year's Lola, on pole at 170.221 mph. The following year Peter Revson, a member of the Revlon cosmetics family who was tragically to die in a Formula 1 accident three years later, upped the ante in his McLaren M16 to 178.696 mph, whereupon Bobby Unser, amazingly, found an extra 17 mph in 1972 with a new Eagle chassis built by the All American Racers team of Dan Gurney. The car owed its roots to the M16, but experienced designer Roman Slobodynskyj had certainly done his homework because Unser topped the speed charts at no less than 195.940 mph.

Development of the engines had also continued, although in fact while the cornering speeds had risen enormously due to the downforce-inducing wings, those same appendages led to an increase in aerodynamic 'drag' which actually caused speeds to drop on the super-speedway straights. The overall outcome, however, was a rapid increase in lap speeds. Confused? Just sit back and think about it for a while; it's really quite logical.

But back to the engines. In the quest for speed, power outputs had risen dramatically, despite the fact USAC had downsized the pure race-bred turbo-charged four-cam engines to 2.65 litres (from 2.8) in 1969. The non-turbo stock-blocks remained eligible at 5.25 litres and non-turbo race-bred engines at 4.2 litres. There was also a new equivalency for turbo-charged stock-blocks at a maximum displacement of 4.2 litres.

The turbo race engines continued to lead the way, however, and bigger turbo-chargers led to more horsepower. The old faithful Offy engine con-tinued to be competitive into the middle 1970s, thanks to a new cylinder head designed by Art Sparks (who along with Goossen and Drake remained as one of the sport's leading engineers for over 40 years). At their peak in 1972, the turbo four-cylinder Offys could produce as much as 1200 bhp – amazing for an engine which could trace its roots way back into the 1920s.

It was with one of these that Jerry Grant, who now heads the competition department for Champion Spark Plugs, became the first man ever to turn a qualifying lap at over 200 mph. He achieved the feat with an Eagle-Offy at Ontario in 1972.

Peter Revson qualified on pole and finished second at Indy in 1971 with Gordon Coppuck's Lotus-inspired McLaren M16.

A year or so later, USAC finally decreed enough was enough. For years a 'pop-off' valve had been used to restrict the amount of manifold absolute pressure (or 'boost') being applied to the engine, and now USAC mandated a boost limit equivalent to 80 inches of mercury. Speeds came down by almost 10 mph. Later, as technology moved forward and power outputs rose again, the limit was restricted to 48 inches and finally to 45 inches, where it remains today.

These restrictions sounded a death knell to the old Offy and its subsequent DGS (Drake-Goossen-Sparks) derivative, which won for the last time at Trenton in 1978, since along with the reduction in boost in 1974 there was also a fuel consumption requirement and another rule which allowed a maximum of forty gallons of fuel (methanol) aboard the cars. The oldy-but-goody simply wasn't efficient enough to compete with the Foyt V8 turbo, which was developed from the 4.2 litre four-cam Ford, and latterly the compact Ford/Cosworth DFX V8 turbo which took over as the powerplant of choice in the late 1970s.

The size and positioning of the wings were also subject to limitations over the years. Nevertheless progress was such that in 1977, former schoolteacher Tom Sneva became the first man ever to post a four-lap qualifying average of better than 200 mph at Indy in one of Roger Penske's McLaren-Ford/Cosworths. Also in 1977, USAC ventured back onto a road circuit, Mosport Park, for the first time since 1970. The following year they got even more adventurous with a foray to England for races at Silverstone and Brands Hatch.

The series in many ways had never been more healthy. The racing was competitive and gaining all the time in international stature. Yet prize money, Indianapolis apart, had not kept pace with the rising costs. The team owners were getting restless. They wanted more of a say in the decision-making process. They felt USAC wasn't pulling its weight; and their fears were heightened when a request to have more representation on the 21-strong Board of Directors was flatly denied.

The result was perhaps the most tumultuous time in the sport's long history. And eventually a mutiny.

Towards the end of 1978, the team owners decided to create their own organization. It was named Championship Auto Racing Teams (CART). Longtime Indy Car entrant U. E. 'Pat' Patrick was elected to be its first president. Other key players in the group's formation included very successful former racers-turned-owners Roger Penske, Jim Hall of Chaparral Cars fame and Dan Gurney. A deal was signed with the SCCA to sanction the events and thereby remain within the jurisdiction of the Automobile Competition Committee for the United States (ACCUS), which itself was governed by the French-based Federation Internationale de l'Automobile (FIA).

The intention behind the formation of CART was to bring the sport to a wider audience and capitalize on what was perceived, rightly, as a huge potential. The owners wanted to be more sympathetic to their own causes while at the same time catering to the needs of the sponsors, the drivers, the circuit promoters, the media and, of course, the spectators. They also set out to provide a more stable rules structure.

The first CART-run race, at Phoenix in March 1979, was won by Gordon Johncock, who narrowly beat Rick Mears in a race broadcast on NBC national network television. It was the precursor to an exciting season in which Mears scored the first of his three titles for Penske Racing. But not everything had been transformed into a bed of roses. Far from it. The Indianapolis Motor Speedway officials didn't trust some of those in charge at the new organization. Instead they continued to side with USAC, creating a rift which even now has yet to be fully bridged.

USAC even tried to bar all of the leading CART teams from competing in that year's Indy 500, on the grounds they were 'not in good standing'. Lawyer John Frasco, later to become CART's chairman, successfully defended the teams in court. They duly took part in the race, with Mears adding insult to injury for USAC by emerging victorious.

USAC doggedly persisted with its own National Championship, headed by the Indy 500, but it drew minimal support. The great A. J. Foyt was crowned as champion for the seventh time in his illustrious career. It was a hollow victory, his rivals consisting mainly of over-the-hill contemporaries from the old dirt track days.

The 1980 season brought some semblance of order with only one champion crowned, although the acrimony continued between USAC and CART. That year also brought the first support from PPG Industries, which has continued to this day as title sponsor of the PPG Indy Car World Series. It was remarkable, too, for the effectiveness of Jim Hall's John

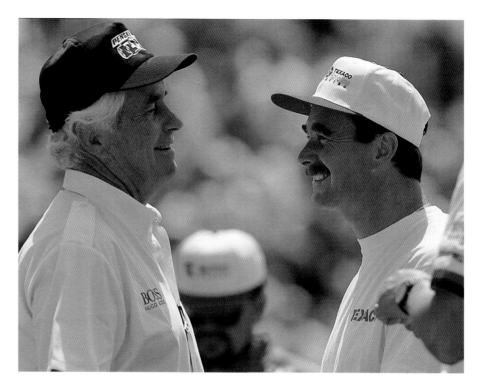

Sharing a joke with Roger Penske, the most successful car owner in Indy Car history. His team had won 71 races prior to this season and the tally continues to rise.

Rick Mears was an absolute master of the ovals before retiring at the end of last season. He is thoroughly enjoying his new role as a coach/mentor to Paul Tracy.

Barnard-designed Chaparral 2K, with which veteran Johnny Rutherford won five races, including Indy, and the PPG Cup crown.

The Chaparral, which had won the final race of the 1979 season in Al Unser's hands, followed the Formula 1 lead (again spearheaded by Chapman's Lotus team) in employing proper 'ground effects', which incorporated the purposeful channelling of air under and over the car to maximize downforce.

A couple of years later, another Formula 1 innovation found its way into the Indy Car ranks. This time it was a new form of chassis construction comprising 'space-age' composite materials, including carbon-fibre, Kevlar and Nomex, which provided great strength and torsional rigidity at minimal weight. The technique, which was first employed by Barnard and McLaren, represented another major breakthrough in Indy car design.

Initially, however, while Formula 1 teams built all-composite chassis from the outset, the Indy car designers relied upon a mix of composite and aircraft-quality aluminium honeycomb, which consisted of a lightweight honeycomb slab bonded together between sheets of high-grade aluminium. The major advantage over all-composite structures was that it would absorb some of the forces in the event of a high-speed impact, whereas composites alone tended to crack. But continued testing and constant development has gradually improved the mix of carbon-fibre and other materials to the extent that it is now capable of withstanding the most staggering impact forces.

The Nigel Bennett-designed Theodore of 1983 was the first Indy car chassis to use a composite top section, riveted onto a 'conventional' aluminium honeycomb 'tub'. Bennett used a similar structure when he switched to Lola in 1984, designing the car with which Mario Andretti claimed his fourth championship title. Composites have been used on all subsequent Indy car designs and undoubtedly their introduction has saved the lives of countless drivers.

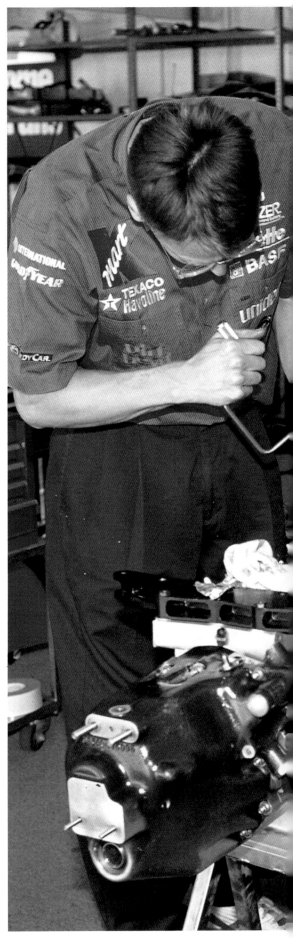

Above The Chevrolet Indy V8/C engine as fitted to Emerson Fittipaldi's Penske PC22.

Right Technology exposed. My spare Lola T93/06 being tended in the garage at Indianapolis.

In recent years, the PPG Cup series has continued to grow in stature. An entente (if not always cordiale) was reached with USAC, which continued to run the Indy 500 and left CART free to develop its own series. The rules have remained stable, which in turn has led to high levels of investment. Technology has marched onwards, with British companies leading the way.

While Cosworth Engineering received no assistance from Ford in developing the DFX motor, Chevrolet decided to enter the fold in 1985. The division of General Motors backed a brand-new V8 engine designed by British-based Ilmor Engineering, which, ironically, at the behest of Roger Penske, had been founded by two ex-Cosworth employees, Mario Illien and Paul Morgan. The engine gradually superseded the aging Cosworth until in the late 1980s it was used by all the top teams.

There have since been several attempts to topple the Chevrolet stranglehold. English engineer John Judd tried valiantly with his Honda-based V8, while Porsche and Alfa Romeo both mounted abortive programs. Porsche and Judd managed a solitary win apiece. The Alfa was a dismal failure. The only American threat to the British steamroller was provided by Buick. Its 4.2-litre turbo stock-block V6 took the top two places at Indy in 1985 and established a new record in 1992 when Roberto Guerrero qualified on pole at a staggering 232.482 mph. Yet it continued to suffer from reliability problems, and its competitiveness in recent seasons has stemmed only from the fact it has been allowed an extra 10 inches of manifold boost pressure at Indianapolis.

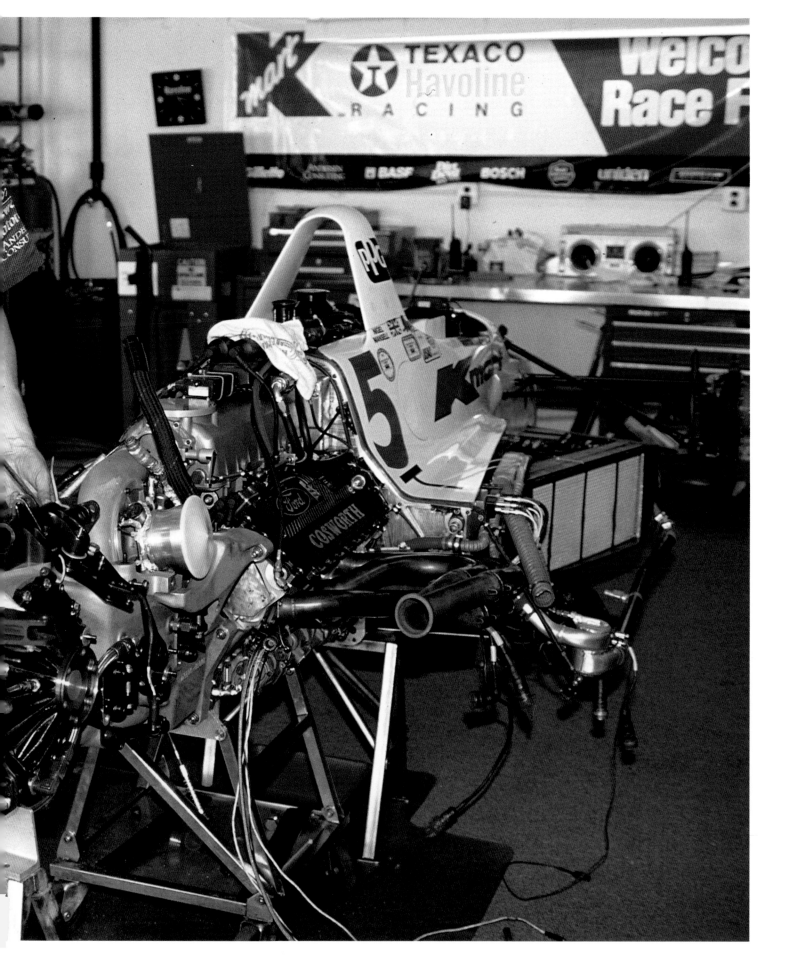

In the meantime, Ford Motor Company and Cosworth Engineering agreed to combine their resources once again to produce the exciting new XB engine, which Mario Andretti and I use in our Newman-Haas Lolas. Meanwhile, Ilmor and Chevrolet have responded to the challenge this year with an all-new Chevrolet Indy V8/C motor, which, like the Ford, is powerful, light and amazingly compact. These two British-conceived and developed engines seem to be very closely matched. Development continues on both, while Honda is one of several Japanese manufacturers which have also expressed an interest in joining in what has developed into an extremely competitive marketplace.

As far as chassis are concerned, the 1980s saw March Engineering come and go in much the same way as the British marque did in Formula 1 some ten years earlier. In 1984, the 33-car grid at Indianapolis comprised no less than 29 Marches. In 1987 there were 28 of the Bicester-built cars in the field. The cars were even more dominant than the Eagles and McLarens had been in the 1970s, rivalling only Harry Miller's virtual monopoly in the late 1920s. But then along came Lola, which claimed the PPG Cup title in 1984, thanks, once again, to Mario Andretti. By the early 1990s it had taken over as the chassis of choice. This season only Penske Cars, whose chief designer, Nigel Bennett, switched across from Lola in 1987, was able to offer a serious challenge; and its cars, too, are built in England, at Poole in Dorset.

For the future, yet another British racing car manufacturer, Reynard, has announced it will challenge the establishment in 1994. It provides not only another example of the depth of the British racing industry but also the esteem with which the PPG Indy Car World Series is now held. It is truly an international sport, quite on a par with Formula 1 in terms of the cosmopolitan array of drivers it has attracted in recent years.

The guidance of the team owners-led CART organization has had much to do with its success. It has fostered a broader outlook than was possible under the old USAC regime. Last year a new record prize fund of $22.9 million was shared among the PPG Cup contestants. Record attendance figures were noted in 12 out of the 16 events.

One reason for the sport's growth has been the appointment of a new president, Bill Stokkan, who arrived in 1990 without a long background in motor racing but with a healthy grasp of business and a positively vibrant enthusiasm for the sport. Stokkan has been responsible for mending some bridges with the world governing body, FISA, as well as at last establishing a fresh rapport with the Indianapolis Motor Speedway.

In 1992 'IndyCar' was introduced as the new brand name for the sport. Later in the year the CART executive board was restructured so that instead of 18 team owners, it now comprises only five members: team owners Roger Penske, Jim Hall, Carl Haas, Dale Coyne and Derrick Walker. In addition, Stokkan and Indianapolis Motor Speedway President Tony George serve as non-voting members.

The more streamlined board has plenty of exciting plans in the pipeline, which include broadening its horizons still further outside the United States. At the same time it is committed to ensuring the series is maintained as a true test of versatility for the drivers. Which in my book accounts for much of its appeal.

Bringing races to the people – 'downtown' Cleveland, Ohio, provides a scenic backdrop for my Kmart/Texaco-Havoline Lola.

This aspect was lacking when it was an all-oval series in the 1970s, but gradually it has returned to encompass virtually every type of race course imaginable. The addition of Cleveland's Burke Lakefront Airport in 1982 represented the start of a trend towards temporary circuits. The defection of Long Beach from Formula 1 to Indy Car in 1984 gave it further momentum. Now there is a healthy mix of short ovals, long ovals, street courses and natural road circuits. Indy Car racing really has a lot going for it. It's a true test of ability.

Which brings us back to the original premise of why motor racing was conceived way back more than 100 years ago: to foster competition; to decide who – or what – was the best, or the fastest. That old adage 'Win on Sunday, Sell on Monday' explains why Ford and Chevrolet are involved in Indy Car racing. Furthermore, the versatility demanded of the drivers is one of the factors which most attracted me to the sport. To win the Indy Car series means a driver has to be competitive on all the different types of venue. That, to me, is a challenge in itself.

How Indy Car Racing Works

What might be described as the 'modern era' of Indy Car racing really began in the autumn of 1978 with the formation of Championship Auto Racing Teams (CART) as a breakaway group from the United States Auto Club (USAC).

It goes without saying that the divorce process ensured some tumultuous times for the sport of Indy Car racing as a whole. The team owners were taking a gamble. If the CART scenario hadn't worked out as anticipated – maybe the race promoters might have taken a stance and sided with USAC, or perhaps the drivers could have reckoned their interests were better served by the existing sanctioning body – then the ramifications could have been disastrous. Of course, the end result has been a resounding success. The sport has prospered in every conceivable way.

I'm not really in a position to compare the way Indy Car racing works with the way Formula 1 operates because obviously I don't know the inner workings of CART as well as I do Formula 1. All I do know is that things are a little bit different. Not necessarily better, but certainly different. CART, for instance, is run more along the lines of a democracy. Each team has been able to provide input towards development of the series. In Indy Car racing one hears a lot of talk about 'the good of the sport' – and I think that's great. Everybody benefits.

It's an interesting conundrum: does a race series profit more from being run democratically or dictatorially, as in the case of Formula 1?

My feeling is that when the regulations are good and the status quo is stable, dictatorship is quite good because no one can argue with it! Sometimes with a democracy you can have too many people on a committee and you can never get an agreement. CART found that out for themselves. The Board of Directors has gone through several changes over the years, the most sweeping of which came in 1992 with the appointment of a more compact seven-man board of directors to make the overall policy decisions based upon recommendations provided by a variety of sub-committees.

Depending on the level of the sport and how the regulations are applied, et cetera, I'm sure there are pros and cons for both forms of government.

I know, too, that there has been talk among the CART fraternity of finding someone to take control of the sport, as Bernie Ecclestone did in Formula 1. If the right figurehead can be found, I don't have a problem with it. But whoever that is would have to be a very special person indeed. He would have to be held in universally high esteem and possess a willingness to understand and not to be able to be swayed one way or another on particular issues for the wrong reasons. He should also be capable of ensuring that all decisions are made 'for the benefit of the sport'. It would be a tough job.

The way CART is structured now, Bill Stokkan, as chairman and chief operating officer of Championship Auto Racing Teams, is the man in overall charge. Nominally, at least. He is the 'figurehead' although, curiously I must admit, he actually does not have a final say in the decision-making process. Bill Stokkan sits in on all the board meetings and provides a great deal of input, but neither he nor fellow board member Tony George, president of the Indianapolis Motor Speedway, are permitted to vote on policies.

Bill Stokkan nevertheless seems to be a good figurehead. He joined CART three years ago after a successful career with Playboy Enterprises Licensing and Merchandising Group. It was at Stokkan's behest that Tony George was invited to join the new slimline CART board, spawning a real hope of ending almost a dozen years of antipathy between CART and the Indianapolis Motor Speedway. He also was responsible for bringing CART back in line with FISA by forging a working relationship with both Max Mosley and the previous FISA president, Jean-Marie Balestre.

The individual team owners meet regularly during the season to exchange views and ideas. Their recommendations are then acted upon by CART's seven-man board of directors, which comprises Bill Stokkan, Tony George and five team owners who were voted into office – Dale Coyne, Carl Haas, Jim Hall, Roger Penske and Derrick Walker. It is their job ultimately to decide which courses of action should be taken.

CART is based in Bloomfield Hills, a leafy suburb of Detroit, Michigan, and also maintains a modest office in New York City from where most of the marketing strategies are formalized. The real 'nuts and bolts' of the organization stems from Bloomfield Hills and is the domain of Kirk Russell. Kirk has been around the Indy Car scene for more than thirty years, starting out on a part-time basis with USAC. He joined CART as technical director upon its formation. In addition to maintaining that role, Kirk has taken on duties as vice president of operations, which means he has his fingers in most of the pies; and if anyone has any queries, Kirk's the man to answer them. I think he does an outstanding job.

Next, effectively, on the totem pole is Wally Dallenbach, an ex-racing driver who is chief steward and director of competition. Wally is based not in the IndyCar office but operates from his home in rural Colorado, high up in the Rocky Mountains. He takes charge during the actual race meetings. Any issues that need resolving are Wally's responsibility. It's his decision to call for a pace car during the race, for example, and he adjudicates any protests that might arise.

Wally is a very honourable man. He doesn't speak with a forked tongue; he tells it as it is. I like that. And if people want to push him to the point

Wally Dallenbach is chief steward and is in charge during race meetings.

Carl Haas has assembled an impressive array of sponsors to keep his team at the forefront of the sport he loves.

where there are grey areas, he has to enforce the regulations as he sees them. He does an outstanding job from that point of view, no question.

A good example stemmed from the race at Detroit in June. I was the fastest qualifier, and so earned the right to pole position on the starting grid, placing me on the inside line for the first corner. But as we came up to the green flag for the rolling start, I was 'jumped' by Emerson Fittipaldi, who had started alongside me on the front row.

In the drivers' briefing before the race, there had been much talk about the start, especially so because on that track there is virtually no opportunity to overtake another car. It's just about impossible. So Wally told us that the pole man, which was me, should lead across the start/finish line at the beginning of the race. He told us he would permit what he called a 'fudge factor' of perhaps a half-a-car length but no more than that. His reasoning was that if Emerson was just nosing ahead as we crossed the line, then at least I would have the opportunity to out-brake him into the first corner. Fair enough. Well, as it happened, Emerson did lead across the line when the green flag waved ... but by about a car's length and a half.

As far as I was concerned, it was a clear-cut issue. He led, I didn't. But I gather there was quite a bit of heated discussion going on behind the scenes. Emerson's team owner, Roger Penske, didn't like it, but eventually Emerson was shown the black flag. Wally decided that he had jumped the start and would have to serve a stop-and-go penalty in the pits. On that track, of course, that effectively put him out of contention for the win. I must admit it was far from a universally popular decision along the pit lane, but given what we'd been told in the drivers' meeting, Wally made the right call. I salute him for that.

Russell and Dallenbach are ably supported by Billy Kamphausen, who seems to be just about everywhere all at once. He's like a little terrier, dashing around and making sure everything runs as it should. Billy looks after all the details. He, Kirk and Wally between them do a very good job.

Of course, as in any sport, there's always some internal politicking, but CART is a tight-knit community – a family almost – so when there are differences, the people concerned are more likely to go into a closed room and sort them out amicably.

Everyone seems to go out of their way to try to help, particularly for any newcomers, as I quickly found out even before my very first race at Surfers Paradise in Australia. When I arrived at the circuit, I went around it several times and was really happy with 99 percent of it. The way the circuit was laid out, with the chicanes, was excellent. But there was one area I wasn't happy with. After taking a few laps in a road car I made up my mind that although I was the new boy on the block, I felt I should mention it to one of the officials. So I did. And he looked at me and thanked me instantly. Then he went to take a look for himself. And less than twelve hours later it was fixed. I was mightily impressed because the changes they made included moving a bunch of four-ton concrete blocks several feet back on one of the corners and then putting some tyres in front of the barrier as well. The Indy Car guys said they were really happy that I should have contributed

Left A rare moment of inactivity for Billy Kamphausen.

Below left The safety features at Surfers Paradise were as comprehensive as any I've seen on a temporary circuit anywhere in the world.

Below The moment of truth during practice at Phoenix. The pyrotechnics were the result of the gearbox exploding upon impact with the wall. Broken parts tend to fly a long way after a crash at over 180 mph.

to the safety of the circuit and encouraged me to feel free at any time, on any circuit we went to, to come forward with any suggestions that might enhance the safety of the drivers or marshals.

That gave me a really, really good feeling – and it certainly helped to increase my own personal comfort zone to know I was dealing with officials with that kind of attitude. It's a great compliment to them, not to me, that they responded in that way.

While I'm on the subject of protection, I should mention one of the series' other great assets: the IndyCar Safety Team. Where Formula 1 has Prof. Sid Watkins, who is on hand at all the races in case of emergency – and before him there was a mobile medical centre first funded by BRM Formula 1 team owner Louis Stanley in the 1970s – CART has Dr Steve Olvey and Dr Terry Trammell who head a fully equipped and staffed medical team, including a superb mobile trauma unit which travels to all the races.

The concept was begun by Carl Horton, who had been involved in the

The IndyCar Safety Team is well
trained and efficient. Notice the
mess at the rear of the car, which
took the brunt of the impact.

manufacturing of emergency rescue and safety vehicles for more than
twenty years. Horton started the project after witnessing a serious con-
flagration in the pits during the 1981 Michigan 500. He took on the
responsibility for assembling all the human and technical resources necessary for a top-flight rescue and medical services crew – and he did a fabulous
job.

Many, many drivers over the years have had cause to be thankful for the
Horton-inspired safety team – myself included. They did everything right
in extracting me carefully from the car I crashed at Phoenix. Then later,
Dr Trammell, who has performed miracles in saving badly broken limbs of
many racing drivers – including Rick Mears, Derek Daly, Jim Crawford,

Jeff Andretti and Nelson Piquet – came down to see me in Florida to make sure I was going to be okay to drive at Indianapolis. I just can't thank him enough.

The expertise of Dr Olvey, who is an Associate Professor of Clinical Neurological Surgery for the University of Miami School of Medicine as well as Director of Neurological Intensive Care at Jackson Memorial Hospital in Miami, and Dr Trammell, who is a partner in Indianapolis Orthopaedics, carries well beyond their medical excellence. Their input has without a doubt contributed enormously to the impressive safety record of the current breed of Indy cars.

Most recently, they recommended that the internal dimensions of the chassis be increased to a predetermined size so that taller, or bigger, drivers should not be unfairly handicapped. At the same time, the larger cockpits afford more room for other protective devices such as additional padding.

I don't think there's any doubt that the safety aspects of Indy Car racing have improved tremendously in recent years. Of course, the cars have to be built well in order to help absorb the immense impacts that can be generated in a crash on a super-speedway oval. The introduction and constant development of high-tech composite materials into chassis construction has minimized the risk of serious injury, while many of the driver aids such as helmets and fire-suits have been pioneered in America by the likes of Bill Simpson, who himself raced an Indy car in the early 1970s.

The regulations are heavily weighted towards improving safety. Last year, for example, there were some freak conditions at Indianapolis with lower-than-expected temperatures. Basically the tyres weren't warming up properly and there were an alarming number of major accidents. Several people got hurt. Badly. Afterwards the teams got together and realized they needed to make the cars stronger. So they mandated an extra few inches of what we call a 'crushable structure', effectively an extension of the integral chassis structure in front of the driver's feet, which was intended to lessen the chance of serious injury to the lower limbs in the event of a head-on crash.

Andrea Montermini spun at Turn One in Toronto after his engine blew up and deposited all its oil underneath his rear tyres (*below*). As his car came to rest against the wall, several other cars tangled together (*top right*), necessitating a full-course caution. The IndyCar Safety Team arrived within seconds (*below right*) to help sort out the mess.

The changes they made to the regulations reflect very well on the series as a whole. The Indy Car body reacted quickly and positively. In years past, the nosecones of the car, the section carrying the front wings, tended to fly off almost instantly, even with a relatively small impact. Now the fixings are probably stronger than on a Formula 1 car. I'm sure that's added significantly to the protection of the driver.

Examples such as this just reaffirm my belief that the people of CART, which includes a large backup team of professional personnel, do a great job in running the series. As with all sports and governing bodies there are grey areas which people try to take advantage of, and at times that causes frustration for the officials and competitors alike. But overall I think CART enforces the rules fairly and allows the drivers and teams to perform at the highest level. My hat's off to them all.

The organization runs smoothly and effectively as a general rule, and a regular race weekend is really quite similar to what I had become used to in Formula 1. With a few small differences, of course. For example, the timing of some of the practice sessions is different; and the time allotted for qualifying is significantly less – there's only 30 minutes instead of one hour in Formula 1, although this year Formula 1 drivers are limited to the number of qualifying laps they can run. For a normal three-day weekend, I always arrive at the track the day before, on the Thursday. That is the same as Formula 1. And my professional approach is identical.

One thing that differs is the promotional side of the sport. I'm required to do far more work out of the car in Indy Car racing than I ever did in Formula 1; but that's partly because instead of having one major sponsor at Newman-Haas Racing we have to service several smaller sponsors – although, of course, they're all very significant in their own right.

Taking Kmart, for example, either Mario or I visit one of their stores the Thursday before each race to sign autographs. Kmart is obviously a big deal. It has 2300 stores in the United States with total sales of something like $33 billion a year.

I'm used to doing presentations, but in Formula 1 they are usually in marquees with specially invited people, not open to the general public. That way it can't get out of hand; but all of our store visits this year have attracted an amazing number of people – many more than they've ever had in the past. The number of people is almost embarrassing. We're supposed to do an hour-long visit but it always ends up being an hour-and-a-quarter or an hour-and-a-half. And then with the travelling time, it more or less turns into a three-hour operation. That can be very tiring but it's another way in which Indy Car racing tries to promote itself to the fans, so it's worth it.

Once I'm at the track, it's pretty much 'situation normal'. I go through the same routines as I would in preparation for a Formula 1 race. It's just a matter of professionalism, making sure I'm as well-prepared as possible. Sometimes one might do things differently for one circuit than another, but

Notice the padding on the right side
of my helmet. It's actually attached
to the side of the cockpit surround
and is there to lend support – as well
as impart a cushioning effect – for
the left handed oval tracks.

perhaps the most difficult thing for me this year is that every circuit is new. Every state I go to is different. I've never been to any of them before. It's the same with the race tracks. The only ones I'd visited prior to the start of the season were Phoenix and Laguna Seca.

In Formula 1 I needed to spend less time preparing for each race because of all the years of experience on the European circuits, both during my formative years and after I'd reached Formula 1. I don't have that advantage in America. Every circuit I go to is new to me, so I have no comfort zone and consequently I'm starting behind the rest of the gang. Almost all of them have raced on each of the tracks, or they've practiced there. Some have been there for a lot of years, others for only a few, but most have been to them sometime or another.

So Indy Car racing is really a whole new adventure. Not only the circuits and the people and the states but the environment and even the culture, because I firmly believe that from among the 50 states which make up America, you can basically look at it as if there were 25 to 30 separate countries. That's how it strikes me. The people are different. The culture is slightly different. So's the climate. There are some very significant distinctions between the various parts of the country. It's a great country to travel around; but it certainly doesn't make my job any easier.

The nice thing, of course, is that at least everyone speaks the same language!

Getting back to the race tracks, there are many parallels between Indy Car racing and Formula 1. If you're a true professional in any sport, you develop a manner, a way of working, and I think you can basically overlap that into different sports and even into other businesses.

Your professional approach is very very important. It can either motivate the people around you, or demoralize them or frustrate them. The response of the Newman-Haas team is second to none. There is a degree of frustration because some of the things we need to get done take perhaps rather more time than we'd like, but really there are no differences there at all between Indy Car racing and Formula 1 as far as I'm concerned.

The times of practice and qualifying are pretty much standardized from race to race, just like in Formula 1. On the Friday there's a 90-minute practice session, which usually runs from 11 am to 12.30 pm, after which the field is split into two groups for qualifying, which runs from 2.30 pm to 3.45. The groups are split according to qualifying times from the previous race. The top half of the field automatically goes into the first group, which runs for half-an-hour, and then, after a 15-minute break to ensure the track is clear, the remainder of the cars go out for their 30-minute session.

It sounds rather complicated but the system works quite well. Splitting the field certainly makes it easier to get a clear lap, although if you've had a problem and end up in the 'slow' group, you can be in trouble.

Also, just as in Formula 1, each driver is allowed two sets of tyres per qualifying session – although again there is an additional concern here because you're only permitted a total of seven sets for the entire weekend. Proper management of tyres can be a critical factor.

On the Saturday, practice is generally from 9 am and runs for an hour. That ensures everyone has to make a pretty early start, but most of the crew members like it because qualifying is all over by 1 p.m., so there's

As each driver takes his turn at qualifying on the ovals, a track official keeps abreast of the lap times and speeds. But don't worry, the entire system is computerized; this is simply for the benefit of anyone in the pit area.

The fuel is topped up and some minor tweaks are made to the suspension settings while I confer with Peter Gibbons during practice in Toronto. This, incidentally, is the spare car, designated by the 'X' below the fuel vent.

That's enough for one day. Practice is over. The tyre pressures are checked as a matter of routine and the Goodyear engineer keeps track of progress. Each car is restricted to only seven sets for race weekend, so tyre management is crucial.

67

plenty of time to get the cars ready for raceday. This time the qualifying groups are split according to the times from the Friday, so you have an opportunity to make it through into the 'fast' group. Also, on Saturday, the quicker guys run last, which means there's often a good battle for the pole which generates a lot of excitement for the crowd.

That's how it works on the road courses. Qualifying on the ovals, though, is completely different. And very difficult. On some tracks this year the schedule has been cut to just one day of practice instead of two, which makes things even more tricky for me because I have even less time to adapt.

Generally we'll have at least two or three practice sessions, during which everyone is out there on the track together, although for qualifying the cars are run one at a time. The team owners draw to determine the qualifying order and the cars are all lined up in echelon on pit lane. It's quite an impressive sight. The atmosphere is intense. When your turn comes up, you're waved out by a marshal just as the previous qualifier is coming into the pits on his cool-down lap. You're allowed to choose between two or three warm-up laps before your qualifying attempt. Then you're shown the green flag as you cross the start/finish line. You have just two timed laps. The fastest one counts as your qualifying time.

One of the major problems in coming to grips with the situation is that after practice in the morning you can wait three or four hours before you go out to qualify. Then you have just one go. That's your lot. It can be very frustrating and disappointing because the weather conditions and the track conditions can change quite dramatically; and if your car isn't right, you've got what you've got and that's it. You don't have a second chance.

It takes quite a bit of getting used to. Your preparation is more or less the same as regular road circuit qualifying but your anticipation and your anxiety is far higher because you've only got one shot. On the road courses at least you've got two 30-minute sessions, so you can adjust the car and hopefully get it how you like it before you decide to go for a quick time; but in this scenario, on the ovals, you just have a one-shot chance. What you see is what you get.

You might think there is a similarity to Formula 1 because in Formula 1 your tyres are usually at their optimum for only a lap or two in qualifying, but the difference is that in Formula 1 you can at least pick the time for your qualifying run. You can go out on the qualifying tyres and if the car's not quite right you can come into the pits, make a change and go back out on that set of tyres. You've got time on your hands to play and adjust. You can think about it. On the ovals you've got no time to think about it and you've got no time to adjust; you've got a one-shot deal, take it or leave it – and if you leave it you're at the back of the grid!

On Sunday morning, raceday, there is a half-hour warm-up session, which most drivers usually use as a final opportunity to run on full tanks, check the systems and make sure everything's as it should be in preparation for the race. If it isn't, that's when the crew starts to panic. Generally, though, there's enough time to change an engine if necessary prior to the race.

While the teams are putting the finishing touches on the cars after the warm-up, we all get together with the chief steward, Wally Dallenbach, for

Marlboro posts a $10,000 award for taking pole position. In addition, if the pole man also wins the race, he is entitled to a $15,000 bonus. Here I am accepting this cheque happily in Australia. If the bonus goes unclaimed, the money rolls over to the next event. Thus, in Cleveland, following six races in which no one else was able to achieve the 'double', Paul Tracy earned a welcome $90,000 reward.

a drivers' briefing. Again it's almost exactly the same as in Formula 1. The briefing gives Wally a chance to go over any details that might be different from other circuits – such as in Detroit where the difficulty in overtaking means that being in the lead at the first corner at the start is even more crucial than usual. He'll talk about the starting procedure. He'll confirm whether or not there will be a mandatory speed limit in the pit lane (which is usually decided the previous day when the crew chiefs have a meeting of their own), and go over any other specific details that might have arisen. He'll also have a word with the less experienced drivers, rag on at them to make sure they use their mirrors and things like that.

In Formula 1 after the drivers' briefing you generally have quite a bit of time to relax, to collect your thoughts before the race. Not so in the Indy Car ranks. Each of the drivers is introduced, one by one, to the crowd. They make the Marlboro pole position award presentation and a whole number of things which are good for the sponsors and the sport. You have less time normally to rest before the race but it's enjoyable and it's another example of the commercial side to Indy Car racing which is a little bit different to Formula 1.

Once this year, in Toronto, we were all paraded around the track for a lap in convertible Chevrolets. It was quite a show. The fans loved it because they had a chance to cheer on their heroes and take a good look at all the drivers. I remember Formula 1 used to be like that a few years ago.

Then it's down to the serious business. Everything is very well orchestrated, right down to the minutest detail, for the benefit of television –

because all the races are televised live around the world. The drivers are ordered to their cars, then you buckle in, make sure the radio's working, and finally comes the command everyone's been waiting for: 'Gentlemen,' or sometimes 'Lady and gentlemen' if Lyn St James is in the field, 'Start your engines!'

It's all a big deal in America, of course, and it certainly gets the heart pumping. After that we all move away from the grid behind the PPG Pace Cars – a collection of garishly painted concept cars maintained by the series sponsors, PPG Industries, and used throughout the weekend not only for official duties but also for ferrying a host of PPG guests and other dignitaries around the circuit during assigned periods on the schedule. All bar the specifically designated pace car – usually driven by three-time Indianapolis 500 winner Johnny Rutherford – pull off after a couple of parade laps, and we do one more lap before he too peels into the pits and we get ready for the 'rolling start.'

It's quite a bit different to the 'standing start' we use in Formula 1 where all the cars are stationary on the starting grid until the green light comes on. What happens in a rolling start is that everyone lines up in two-by-two grid order, as determined by qualifying times, and runs at the same pace as the pole position car. The drivers have to maintain position until the official starter, Jim Swintal, decides the time is right to throw the green flag. We're usually in second gear at that point, sometimes first, and as soon as the green waves, we're off.

It sounds quite straight-forward, doesn't it? But believe me there's more to it than meets the eye. In my first race at Surfers Paradise I qualified on

Below The atmosphere builds as my car is towed into its position on the starting grid in front of the main grandstand in Milwaukee.

Above The marshal is attempting to signify there's an incident on the inside of the exit of the corner, out of sight to oncoming drivers, and indicating we should take the outside line to avoid the mêlée.

pole but found myself too close behind the pace car when it pulled off into the pit lane. I had to lift off the throttle momentarily just when I needed to punch it, which gave Fittipaldi an opportunity to jump ahead of me.

We've had a few, let's say, 'interesting' starts this year, but suffice to say that if Jim Swintal waves the green, it's a go. If he doesn't like the way in which the cars are lined up, he waves the yellow flag. In that case we have to do a complete extra pace lap – which counts towards the race distance – before trying it all again.

To be honest, that's simplifying the matter slightly, because there are a few weird scenarios that can occur; but to describe exactly how and where and if and why, I tell you, I could write a book on that alone.

The start itself is when you first really notice the difference between Indy Car racing and Formula 1. And once the race gets under way there are a lot more things you have to pay attention to. Things like full-course yellows, pace cars, blend lines, pit stops and refuelling come into play along with all sorts of other parameters which do not exist in Formula 1.

A 'local yellow' means a yellow warning flag will be displayed by the marshals – or corner workers as they're called in America – at one particular corner. That's a normal procedure around the world, Formula 1 included. The yellow is used to alert the drivers to some sort of incident up ahead. It might be a spin by another car or some debris on the track. When the yellow is waved, no one is allowed to overtake.

An American-style full-course yellow will come about as the result of a more serious incident on the circuit. For example, a crash where a car may be stranded on the track and cannot be removed without endangering the marshals. In that situation the chief steward will activate the pace car driver who is on stand-by throughout the entire race, usually parked near the pit lane exit. The pace car will then go out onto the track and its driver will position himself in front of the race leader. All the other cars are obliged to slow down and run in line astern behind the leader.

When the pace car is out on the track often provides a good opportunity to make a pit stop. And in most instances the cars will require at least two pit stops during a regular 200-mile race. The reason for that is because each car is restricted to running a 40-gallon fuel tank. And the cars must maintain a fuel consumption of 1.8 miles per gallon. Each car is allocated enough methanol on that basis, so everyone starts the race with an allotment of around 111 gallons. Obviously the precise amount varies according to the exact race distance.

The car will have a full quota of 40 gallons on board at the start, having been filled to the brim by the official Valvoline truck on the starting grid. The remainder is deposited in each team's refuelling rig along pit lane. It is up to each team to determine how best it will use its fuel allocation, but for obvious reasons it will be advantageous to minimize the pit stops. And it follows that you will lose less ground if you can pit under a full-course caution because everyone is running much slower and the chance of being lapped by the race leader is considerably reduced.

When it's time for a pit stop – and I'll go into more detail about the timing in a moment – you have to pay attention to what are known as the 'blend lines,' which are perpendicular markings across the track at the entrance and exit to the pit lane. If you come in for a pit stop under a full-course caution and you're following the pace car, you're not allowed to pass the pace car until you're in the pit lane and across the blend line. More importantly, when you come out of the pits, if you reach the blend line before the pace car does, you're entitled to go on around the track and rejoin the tail of the field. If the pace car beats you to the line, then you must fall in behind it. According to the letter of the law, if there is a line of cars already following the pace car, no one is obliged to let you into the line. You have to sneak in wherever you can. Normally, though, a gentleman's agreement comes into effect and you'll 'blend' in to the pack of cars appropriately.

If you violate the blend line laws, or if you overtake under a local yellow, or you're caught exceeding the speed limit in the pit lane, the usual form of admonishment takes the form of a 'stop-and-go' penalty. In that case the driver will be required to come into his pit stall, bring the car to a halt, and then go on his way again.

It's a time-consuming business. I was assessed a stop-and-go penalty in Australia for passing another car while a yellow flag was being waved in one of the corners. I honestly never saw the yellow, and sometimes in the heat of a battle it is difficult to see the warning flags. In any case apparently I passed another car so I was penalized. And by the time you have slowed down to come into the pits, come to a stop and then built up speed again, you will have lost valuable time. The chances are, too, that you had to work hard on the track to make up that time in the first place, so it can be very very frustrating.

Chief Steward Wally Dallenbach is the one who makes the decisions upon hearing a report from another official out on the track or in the pits. Wally then will broadcast the penalty over the published Indy Car radio frequency which is monitored by all the officials and by the teams. Another official in pit lane will be dispatched to impart news of the penalty to the relevant team manager, although chances are he'll already be aware of the situation from the original radio transmission. The teams themselves are responsible for calling their drivers into the pits for a penalty. In addition, the official flagman, Jim Swintal, will often display a black flag along with the appropriate car number which as in Formula 1 means that car must proceed immediately to the pits.

As I said, there's a lot to pay attention to. And even if you don't get caught out with a penalty, it's critical to make your pit stops at the right time. That's why it's very very important to have a team manager who's well versed and experienced to be able to cope with all the different scenarios. A good team manager can win or lose a race just as easily as the driver, and that's why the Newman-Haas team is very fortunate in having Jim McGee.

Jim has been around forever, it seems. He worked with legendary Indy Car chief mechanic Clint Brawner on Mario Andretti's car when Mario won his first (and so far only) Indy 500 in 1969, and in the '70s was an integral part of Roger Penske's operation. Jim led Penske Racing to its first National Championship title with Tom Sneva in 1977, then switched across to manage Pat Patrick's team. His experience and savvy helped Emerson Fittipaldi to win the 1989 PPG Cup, while last year he was team manager for Bobby Rahal's title-winning effort prior to joining Newman-Haas. Jim and I are in permanent radio contact during the race. He passes on all sorts

Below I'm prepared to go on record as saying Jim McGee is one of the best team managers I've had in my career.

The field was well spread out for a restart early in the race at N.H.I.S., although I'm under pressure from Raul Boesel. Scott Goodyear and Paul Tracy head the pursuit.

Overleaf A typical pit stop will entail a change of tyres and replenishment of fuel through the gravity-fed rig. Only six men are allowed 'over the wall'. In addition, a pit marshal stands behind the car with a fire extinguisher at the ready. Notice that the outside tyre changers carry the fresh rubber with them, while the inside tyres are held in position by helpers behind the pit wall. If I need a drink, a bottle is proffered by means of a long pole. It's a well-orchestrated routine that generally is completed in around 15 seconds.

of information and I rely on him very heavily.

If it's what we call a 'green race', by which I mean there are no caution (full-course yellow) periods, I make the calls concerning pit stops because I manage the fuel in the car. I keep tabs on how much fuel I have left and I will stay out on the track for as long as I can before making a pit stop. The computerized on-board data system displays a read-out on the automated dash panel to tell me how much fuel I have in hand, and I will keep going until I see a pre-determined number that we agree before the race. If there's a full-course yellow, however, and if it's within the window of parameters for refuelling and we can still make it to the finish without having to stop again, Jim will make the call. I believe that's the way it works for every team up and down the pit lane.

At each pit stop, aside from topping up with methanol, we usually take on a fresh set of Goodyear Eagle radial tyres. I will often get a quick drink, too, from a water bottle which is passed across from behind the pit wall on a long pole. Anyone who has seen an Indy Car pit stop will have noticed one more difference from Formula 1, because in Indy Car racing we are limited to just six guys going 'over the wall' to help service the car rather than 12 or more which take part in a regular Formula 1 tyre stop.

Each crewman has a designated task. Generally there is one man to change each wheel, with one operating both the air-jack to raise the car off the ground and the fuel vent, which evacuates air from the fuel tank as the methanol is replenished. Another is in charge of the refuelling nozzle. It's a well-orchestrated routine. The guys practice for hours back in the workshop and generally the car will be back down off the jacks and back into the race in around 14 or 15 seconds.

The pit stops tend to make things very very exciting. Both for the fans and the drivers. Strategy can be extremely important. Above all, though, the way the series is run I have to say is always for the betterment of the sport and with safety very much in mind. I think the officials are to be very highly commended for that.

The pit stops and the penalties and the cautions add an extra dimension to the racing. Of course, the most difficult part of any race is being quick enough to win, but there's so much else to think about, too.

If you're quick enough to be competing at the front, you still have to manage your fuel load properly. You also have to look after your tyres. The Goodyears are of a very significantly harder compound than in Formula 1, primarily due to the extra weight of the Indy cars, and they go 'off', by which I mean they become far less effective as they wear. They produce less grip. The car invariably starts slip-sliding away.

The tracks are so varied – from short ovals to super-speedways to street circuits to road circuits – that the parameters within which the car has to be set up are very very wide, and because of this you have to have an enormous array of knowledge. You have to pay closer attention to the climatic conditions you're racing under and understand how the varying conditions will affect the car – which they surely do, especially on the ovals.

You have to think about the specific demands of each track, depending on how difficult it is to overtake. There's no question you'll encounter a lot more traffic in an Indy Car race than in Formula 1, so you have to pay attention to how and where you can overtake. Because of that, the way you

set up the car aerodynamically becomes vitally, vitally important.

You have to pay close attention to the track conditions, too, because on virtually every circuit I've been to there have been several corners where the surface starts breaking up halfway through the race. This throws a spanner in the works, as we say, because it will seriously affect the way the car handles.

In Formula 1, I always said to my engineer that initially, if I could, within 20 laps, I'd like to build up a 10-second lead; and if we were planning to make a pit stop, I'd try and stretch that to 20 seconds before the pit stop. That way, even if we had a rough pit stop, we should by rights still emerge in the lead.

That would be a perfect scenario, if you make a copybook start and ran a clockwork race, but 99 times out of 100, of course, that doesn't happen. In Indy Car racing, though, there are all these different parameters to take into account. They all have to be computed and programmed into the brain whereby you literally attack the race and then adjust your position as you go along, according to where you are and what circumstances might arise. If you have a problem, you have to react accordingly.

You have to decide how hard to push; when to charge and when to be conservative. You can't just charge from the start and keep on charging because chances are you'll burn up your tyres – or your fuel, or both – so you won't have anything left for the end of the race. In addition to that, there's always the spectre of a full-course caution. If you've busted your behind, as the Americans say, to pull out a big lead, that can be eradicated in a moment when the yellow flags wave. And if you've pushed too hard, too soon, you might not have enough left in the car for the remainder of the race. As I say, there's a lot to think about.

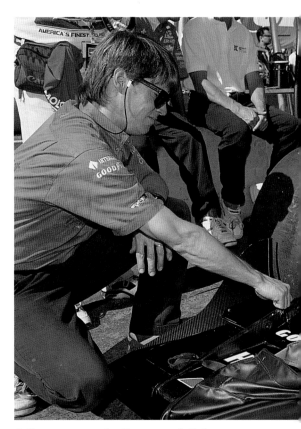

Adjustments to the front aerofoils by Jerry Bouschard (*above*) and the rear wing by Trevor Weston (*right*) can be completed in a few seconds. Note the shrouds to deter prying eyes.

To some extent you have to bear in mind the points situation, too. The system of scoring is somewhat different to Formula 1 which awards points to the top six finishers on the basis of 10-6-4-3-2-1. Thus by finishing, say, in third place you earn less than half of the winner's tally. In Indy Car racing, more of a premium is placed on consistency. Points are awarded down to 12th place. The winner earns 20 points, with the remainder credited as follows: 16-14-12-10-8-6-5-4-3-2-1. In addition, the pole position qualifier is awarded an extra point, as is the driver who leads most laps in the race. The bonuses reward outright pace, which to my way of thinking is entirely appropriate.

The Indy Car series has developed into a finely tuned and ultra-competitive form of racing in recent years. I think it's true to say that the series is probably more wide-open now than at any time in the last 30 or 40 years. Costs have risen, of course, and the team owners are constantly seeking ways in which to maintain the budgetary constraints within reasonable bounds, but it still costs a heck of a lot less money to compete in Indy Car racing than it does in Formula 1.

That is due in large part to the regulations themselves. CART has gone out of its way to limit the space-age technology whereas Formula 1 *is* the pursuit of technical excellence. Until now, innovation has been the name of the game, whether it's hydraulics, computers, electronics, aerodynamics or whatever. In Indy Car racing, by contrast, the rules are set and they're standardized from year to year. There's obviously more control, which is

concentrated on trying to contain the escalation of costs. This year, for example, the IndyCar board outlawed traction-control systems, which had been introduced last season. Automatic transmissions, 'fly-by-wire' throttle mechanisms and active suspension are banned. And that's fine.

The last few years have been very difficult for Formula 1. The technological steps, the breakthroughs, have been enormous. And very impressive. And hugely expensive. They have also made government of the sport sometimes very difficult. That's not a criticism of any sort; it's just another example of how the two series differ. Indy Car racing is a lot simpler. It's very much like Formula 1 was five or six years ago – and that's not to put this formula down. Quite the opposite. I think that's a credit, a compliment, and the owners have to be careful to regulate the series, otherwise costs will escalate further.

There is some criticism that the regulations are perhaps too regimented and too restrictive, that there's not enough room for development or innovation, but I don't think this is valid. Not from the point of view of either cost or competition. The regulations achieve good, fair racing at a competitive price; and I think if people lose sight of that, they're losing sight of what the formula is all about.

You just have to look at the quality of the racing, the number of different winners, to realize how good the regulations are as they stand. There will always be favourites going into every race, but if they fall by the wayside, which they surely do from time to time, there are always 'dark horses' who can come through to win on occasion. Again, it just shows that the cars and the engines are very, very well matched.

One of the other great things about Indy Car racing is that you can be a small team or a big team and still compete at the highest level because all the cars are customer cars. Anyone can go out and buy a Lola chassis or a Ford/Cosworth engine just like mine. You can buy the latest Chevrolet/C engine. Next year Reynard will be producing customer cars too. So there are no excuses. What that means basically is that the difference between winning and losing is down to the team and the driver. Therefore, it's not going to matter whether you have 20 or 30 or 70 million dollars to spend on research and development; that's not going to make a difference on whether you are going to be competitive or not. Again, that's purely and simply down to the regulations and that's why I'm such a great supporter of this formula.

Indy Car racing is thoroughbred racing and it provides great racing. The cars are extremely competitive, they are reasonably technologically advanced and they put on a great show. Isn't that what this sport is all about?

First Impressions of Indy Racing

*T*he first Indy Car race I ever witnessed firsthand was at Laguna Seca, California, in October 1992. It was the final race of the season and I must say, I was impressed. I couldn't help but notice right away how competitive it was and how professional some of the teams were; and also how friendly and admirable the whole atmosphere seemed to be.

The people were so accommodating. They all seemed to get along so well. There was still a good healthy rivalry between the various teams, plenty of needle, but without the petty back-biting and jealousies that, regrettably, seem to have permeated the European racing scene. Everyone has a job to do, just like in any form of motor racing – and life, come to that – but what struck me at Laguna Seca was how everyone was openly trying to help one another to achieve that job. To me that was very, very important and very gratifying.

I was also really surprised how warmly I was accepted by the American fans – and by the media too, I should say. It made quite an impression on me. It made me even more excited about the switch I'd made in my career and gave me even more to look forward to than I'd bargained for. There was no doubt in my mind I'd made the right decision so far as my future was concerned.

In some ways, of course, it wasn't easy to leave Formula 1, but at least I had the satisfaction of knowing I left while I was at the very top, which is something very few people can say they've done. I've had thirty Grand Prix wins, I've won the World Championship and I've had some wonderful times. If you're going to make any sort of change in your life, that's the best way to make it – while you're at the top.

At the same time, when you are at the top, experiencing the best there is, you don't want to let your standards fall. And again I was quite fortunate, because my new Indy Car team, Newman-Haas Racing, is a fantastic racing team. It's well-structured, well-organized, well-funded and well-equipped. And the people there are second to none.

It's one of the main reasons I decided to compete in the Indy Car series. Motivation, you see, is a critical aspect in the make-up of any racing driver. He (or she) has to be motivated to realize the full potential of both himself

My crew chief, Tom Wurtz (*left*), is deep in thought as crewman Jim Volini drives the pit cart back to the transporter following practice at Long Beach.

and his equipment. And my motivation comes from being given the opportunity to drive at the highest level – the level that you feel you need not just to compete but to win – and then go on to win another championship.

My motivation didn't come from a desire simply to race in the Indianapolis 500, even though it is the greatest sporting event in the world; my motivation was fired by the possibility of winning the Indy Car championship and trying to be the first Englishman ever to have achieved that. Because, of course, several of my predecessors had switched across from Formula 1 and won odd races, even the Indianapolis 500, but no one had ever won the championship.

And now, thanks to Paul Newman and Carl Haas, I have that opportunity to perform at the highest level, perhaps to win a championship. It's what spurs me on. I love driving and I love winning. That's where my inspiration comes from.

I think it goes without saying that I was really looking forward to getting started in my new life as an Indy Car driver. But after attending that first race at Laguna Seca, my next real contact with the Newman-Haas team wasn't until we started testing early in the New Year. In between times I took a little time off to have some minor surgery to correct a problem with my left foot.

The injury actually stemmed from a karting accident many years ago, although it didn't really bother me until it was aggravated in a crash I had in Australia in 1991. Some of the small bones in my foot weren't matched properly. I needed to have some bone tissue removed. It was a relatively minor operation, although it was complicated slightly by an infection I

'Come on, bring us your expertise,' team co-owners Paul Newman and Carl Haas told me. 'You'll enjoy it. It'll be less work...'

Preparing to take the '92 Lola-Ford/Cosworth out for the first time at Firebird Raceway on January 4.

somehow picked up. In any case it really didn't set us back too much, and I'm glad I had the work done because now, for the first time in several years, I can walk properly.

Once that was out of the way, my next priority, and that of the team, was to get organized for the new season. Obviously we needed to conduct an extensive testing campaign in order to ease the transition from one formula to another. If you want to be competitive, to be the best, you must do your homework, as in any walk of life – it doesn't come for free no matter what team you go to – and it certainly helped being a part of such a professional outfit as Newman-Haas Racing. And homework in motor racing means testing.

I noticed right away how well the team gelled. My race engineer, Peter Gibbons, had worked with Michael Andretti for the previous couple of seasons. He was also with Michael at Kraco Racing, right at the start of Michael's Indy Car career, so they had built up a very strong relationship. In the meantime Peter had spent a few years with Penske Racing, primarily working with Rick Mears. So his credentials were impressive. We got along well right from the start. Peter is also from England originally, although he's spent most of his life in the States. We talk the same language – and, when I say that, I'm referring to the way in which we communicate about matters concerning the car.

It's the same with Mario's race engineer, Brian Lisles. He, too, is an Englishman. He first cut his teeth, so to speak, in Clubmans' racing. Before that he worked as an engineer in the steel industry. Brian worked for the Tyrrell Formula 1 team for several years before moving State-side to join

Peter Gibbons, my race engineer, has been a tremendous help this season in helping me get used to a totally new set of surroundings.

Carl Haas and Paul Newman's team. The thing about Brian is that he's very methodical, very analytical, and very intelligent. He and Peter make an excellent combination, which I'm delighted to be able to take advantage of. They certainly make my job easier.

We all started out working together with a lengthy test session in Arizona in early January. The first track we went to, Firebird Raceway, is situated right outside the town of Chandler only a few miles to the south of Phoenix, the largest city in Arizona. Despite that, the track makes you feel like you're in the middle of the desert. It's what I would term a traditional road course, except the edge of the track is bounded by sand and scrub. There are some of those huge distinctive cactus plants right across the road.

It's only a short track and it's used exclusively for testing. Business is obviously pretty good, too, especially in the winter months because you can generally rely on the weather being nice. (You can forget the place in the summer months, though, because more often than not the temperatures are well over 110 degrees – and they tell me you have to watch out for the rattle-snakes. No thank you!) In any case, several different track layouts are available at Firebird and they tend to be heavily booked.

We went out in the '92 Lola for my first test, leaving my teammate Mario

I remember Brian Lisles from when he used to work in Formula 1 with the Tyrrell team. His hair turned white before he started working with Mario!

Andretti to shake down the brand-new '93 car. That was obviously the smart thing to do. I had nothing to gain from driving the new car since I didn't have anything to relate it to. This way I could gain a taste for what I was letting myself in for, while Mario, with his wealth of experience, could concentrate on gaining an insight into what would be our race car for the season ahead.

Surprisingly perhaps, my initial impression was that the Indy car wasn't that much different from the Formula 1 cars I'd been used to. You still had to pay attention to the same sort of things. Having said that, there were several fundamental differences. The most noticeable for me was the fact the Lola didn't have an automatic gearbox. So for the first time in four and a half years I had to use the gear-shift. Boy, was that tricky! Even my own road cars are automatic these days. I'd become thoroughly spoiled and lazy.

I took quite some time to get my left foot and my right hand synchronized again, and the transition wasn't any easier because the last time I used a manual shift in Formula 1 there were six or seven gears to play with. At first, I couldn't remember which gear I was in; then I couldn't coordinate my left leg properly to use the clutch. I kept telling my crew the clutch was dragging, whereas in fact I wasn't even depressing the clutch pedal. I felt pretty silly. It took a good half-dozen laps to get any kind of feel for it, and of course I had to remember how to heel-and-toe all over again too. It was really quite an interesting time.

The next thing I noticed was how much heavier the Indy car was than a Formula 1 car. Outwardly, at first glance, the two cars seem very similar, but the regulations for the two formulae are quite different. The minimum weight of a Formula 1 car, for example, is 505 kgs, or 1113 lbs, whereas an Indy car must top the scales at 1500 lbs, or 680 kgs. That's quite a significant discrepancy. And the primary reason is because the Indy car has to race on all sorts of different types of track, not just road courses as in Formula 1. And as you can probably imagine – and as I know from painful first-hand experience – an impact with a concrete wall at even 180 mph, let alone 230 mph at Indianapolis, bears absolutely no comparison whatsoever with any accident a Formula 1 chassis might have to absorb.

The extra weight is very, very significant. It makes it much harder to change direction. When I first drove my Lola-Ford/Cosworth, I found I had to brake much earlier than with a Formula 1 car, both because of the extra weight and the fact the car had steel brakes instead of the carbon fibre brakes I'd been used to in Formula 1. Consequently there were a few differences in technique I needed to work out.

To be quick in a Formula 1 car, you have to drive it on a knife-edge; you have to wring the car by its neck, so to speak. There's a very fine line between riding on the edge of adhesion through a corner and spinning – as I think Michael Andretti has been finding out after switching to Formula 1 this year. Of course, one could say that about any racing car, but with an Indy car there are some additional concerns because of the extra weight and the lack of carbon brakes. If you try to drive an Indy car the same way you drive a Formula 1 car it will bite you – especially on the ovals. The two cars react quite differently.

I'll give you an example: with a Formula 1 car the carbon brakes enable you to go incredibly deep into the corners, and if you miss an apex a little bit you can sometimes make a correction and effectively take a second bite at the apex – or the cherry as you might call it. But that's a lot more difficult to do with an Indy car because it's almost 400 lbs heavier and there's a lot more weight to transfer.

In some ways you have to be more precise with the Indy car. If you miss the apex and you need to turn more sharply to try to clip that apex, the car, because of its weight, is slower to react. So therefore you lose more time.

That was just one of the things I had to file away in my head, my own on-board computer. I had to detach myself from what I'd been used to in the past in Formula 1 and say, hang on, this car's a lot heavier; it's going to react differently.

Another thing I had to get used to again was the turbo-charged Ford/Cosworth XB V8 engine. It's quite different to the normally aspirated Renault V10 I'd been using in Formula 1. The actual power felt about the same – somewhere in the region of 750 horsepower – but again, because the Indy car's so much heavier, it feels just a little more sluggish coming off the corners. There is some turbo-lag but nothing like the amount we used to have when we ran the big-boost turbo engines in Formula 1. Once you're up to speed, though, and the turbo kicks in, it's a really great feeling.

The tyres, too, are different. The Indy cars run on Goodyear Eagle radials, just like in Formula 1, but the construction of the tyres is different and the rubber compound is quite a bit harder in Indy Car racing – again that's primarily due to the weight of the cars – and therefore they have a lot less grip.

So, as I say, there were a lot of things to get used to during that first test

Below Crew man puts the finishing touches to a Ford/Cosworth engine before it goes into the car.

Right Goodyear provide all the tyres in Indy racing. Each car is allowed seven sets of tyres each race weekend.

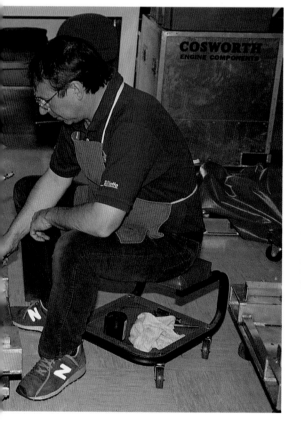

My first test on the oval at Phoenix International Raceway. Paul Newman, Brian Lisles and Carl Haas look on anxiously, while team manager Jim McGee, wearing the headset, prepares to log the lap times.

at Firebird Raceway. But everything went well. We ran for a whole day and a little more and I hadn't even spun the car yet. We'd clocked up quite a few miles, and after I began to feel comfortable I radioed in to Peter Gibbons and the guys to tell them I was going to do a 'spin test'.

I couldn't help noticing it went quiet all of a sudden. I don't think they really knew what I was talking about. But it's something I've done several times before. It's just another way to learn a bit more about the car, gain some insight into how it reacts to full throttle.

I just told them not to worry, I'm going to do this deliberately, just chuck the car around and play with the throttle while the car's spinning. It's quite fun – and I'm sure it's quite spectacular to watch – but what you do is chuck it around in controlled conditions to try to learn a little more about the limits of the car.

That's fine at Firebird, because there's nothing to hit. I did it at the end of the back straight where there's plenty of run-off area. I also made sure the guys on the crew could see it, because I felt pretty sure they'd get a kick out of it. The only problem was, after I'd done about six consecutive spins, there was so much tyre smoke I couldn't see where I was going. I was a little disorientated, so when I straightened up the car and emerged from the smoke, I ended up being off in the dirt. I don't know whether you can picture it, but basically, the track was over there somewhere and I was over here!

We ended up running for two days at Firebird. Mario was there for one day too, shaking down the new '93 Lola chassis for the first time. Then his part of the team packed up and moved across the other side of town to Phoenix International Raceway (P.I.R.), to continue testing on the one-mile oval. We were planning to join him that afternoon but we had a few problems. We were doing some turbo testing and it took a little bit longer than we had anticipated; but we had a good test. It was a good familiarization for me. We also did some chassis testing and some engine testing, so we were able to move forward on development.

The only problem was that when we finally moved over to P.I.R. for my first oval test the weather had turned against us. It was tipping down with rain. Really miserable. It felt like a typical wet English day, to be honest. The only difference was that, of course, in America they don't run on the ovals.

I kept joking with the guys, asking where the wet tyres were. I said I'd go out on wets, just to have a look, but I wasn't being serious. There's absolutely no way you could run on an oval in the wet. It would be suicidally dangerous – and believe me, the ovals are quite daunting enough in the dry.

We sat around for the whole morning. Michael Knight, who coordinates all the public relations activities for Newman-Haas Racing, had publicized the fact we'd be testing in Phoenix, so a huge army of journalists and television crews turned up to watch. It was an incredible gathering. I think every British daily newspaper was represented, including a bunch of people I'd known from the Formula 1 days, plus quite a few from the American press turned up. Several people told me there were more properly accredited media representatives at that test than they've ever seen there for the race.

The rain was annoying because it took away valuable testing time, but it did give the journalists a good opportunity to get some one-on-one inter-

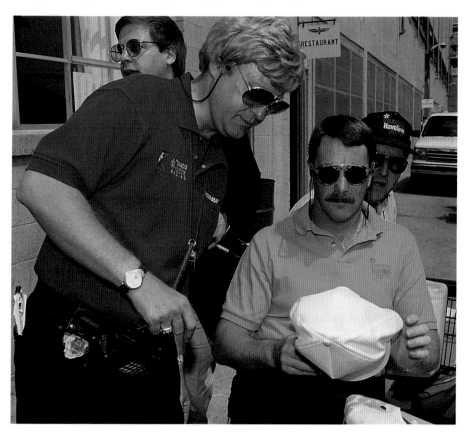

Michael Knight lends a hand at Indianapolis as we get ready for yet another press conference.

views. It also gave me a chance to get to know a few of them. So from that perspective it worked out okay. I entertained some of them by giving rides around the track, so that gave them something to write about too.

After lunch, the rain finally stopped and the track started to dry out. There was a bit of a breeze from the west and that really helped. Actually, it was amazing how quickly the surface dried, and we were able to get out there by about 3.30 in the afternoon. Conditions still weren't too good – in fact, Bobby Rahal, who was due to be sharing the track with us, didn't bother to go out at all – but at least I was able to get some running in. It went pretty well, and I think a lot of people were surprised at how quickly we were able to go. I ran a total of 70 laps that first afternoon, and at the end of the day I was able to do two consecutive laps at 21.4 seconds. That's an average speed of 168.22 mph. The time would have been good enough to place me fourth on the grid for the previous year's race at Phoenix, so it goes without saying I was pretty pleased.

We weren't running as much boost as we could have. At the same time Peter Gibbons deliberately engineered some understeer into the car just to be on the safe side, because the last thing you want on an oval – especially when you're totally lacking in experience, as I was – is oversteer. Furthermore, the track was a bit damp at the top which made it a bit iffy. So all in all, I was absolutely thrilled and delighted with what we were able to do. Everyone seemed to be pretty impressed. Having said that, it's all credit to the team because they did a fantastic job. They knew exactly what settings to put on the car in terms of aerodynamics, springs, shock absorbers, roll-bars, roll-centres and everything else. Driving the car was the easy bit. It was perfectly set up. The balance was just great.

A lot of people asked me what it was like to drive on the oval for the first time, and while my first impression stressed the importance of having a good team behind you, to give you a car that inspires confidence, I had to say it didn't compare with anything else I'd ever done in my life. Oh, boy, it was a huge difference. There's just nothing like it.

One of the biggest things I had to get used to was hanging onto the car in a straight line. Seriously. Because the car is set up to turn into left-hand corners all the time. When Stefan Johansson switched to Indy Car racing from Formula 1 the year before I did, he took one look at his car before he drove it for the first time on an oval and said: 'That car looks like it's had an accident already – and I haven't even sat in it yet!'

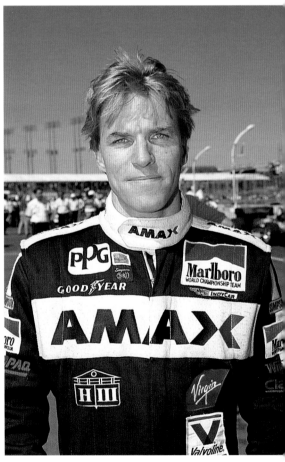

And he's right. For example, the wheel cambers are set negative on the right side and positive on the left side. It looks really silly when you see it for the first time, with the car leaning over to one side. Then there's tyre stagger to take into consideration, where the right-rear tyre is slightly larger than the left-rear. When you sit down and think about it logically, it all makes sense: the car only has to turn left and you're trying to help it as much as you can. Oval track racing really has developed into a science. There's a heck of a lot to learn.

In any case, I found it hard to describe that first experience at Phoenix, and still do. I had trouble finding the words to express the sensations. But it was fascinating, it was an incredible challenge and it was certainly very, very exciting – more so than I had anticipated. When making the switch from Formula 1 to Indy cars, you can compare road courses with Formula

Above The weather conditions weren't too good at P.I.R. Bobby Rahal ran only a few laps before departing for the day. Bobby, like me, is an avid golfer. I think I know where he was that afternoon . . .

Left Stefan Johansson drove for Ferrari and McLaren during his Formula 1 days. Now he is an accepted member of the Indy Car ranks, albeit still seeking his breakthrough victory.

1; but it's not worth even trying to compare an oval to Formula 1. It's another world. And I tell you, it feels quick! It really holds your attention. It's incredibly exhilarating.

The team were wonderful, especially Mario, who took me round the circuit and showed me some of the pitfalls before I went out. That certainly helped give me a little bit of confidence. And the engineers: I would hate to go to an oval for the first time and not be properly prepared. It would be a terrifying experience.

In my case, having been a thoroughbred road racer throughout my career, visiting the oval for the first time added a new dimension, a new plateau to racing. The real key to being quick, I found, was to carry your speed all the way around on the oval. You have to be smooth and, believe me, that's easier said than done. It's really, really tough, and again I was lucky because I was able to benefit from the enormous experience of Mario Andretti and the Newman-Haas team.

Their input and their encouragement helped enormously in terms of improving what I call my 'comfort zone' on the ovals. When I first started, my comfort zone was zero. I felt just like a fish out of water. But with the team behind me, setting up the car based on all the knowledge they've gained with Mario (and also with Michael) and doing all the hard work behind the scenes, they were able to inspire me, give me the confidence I needed to expand my comfort zone. They're unquestionably the ones who deserve all the credit.

As for myself, when I first arrived in Phoenix – and again when I finally went to Indianapolis for the first time – I really had no idea what to expect. I just tried to keep a completely open mind. The primary reason for that was because a lot of people, as a result of their own prejudices, were trying to persuade me not to come over here last year. They gave me the most gruesome details, telling me how terrible America was and all the rest of it – especially the oval racing. They were obviously saying all those things for their own reasons, but I decided I was going to go there and do the best job I could. And, of course, most things have worked out just fine.

The biggest thing for me, and for Rosanne, is that we've been made to feel so welcome in America. I noticed it when I visited that first race at Laguna Seca. Everyone bent over backwards to make me feel at home. They even arranged for me to keep my number, Red Five.

I had that number for several years in Europe. It became almost synonymous with me, in much the same way as '27' became attached to the memory of the late, great Gilles Villeneuve. I was privileged enough to run number 27 when I was with Ferrari. It was a great feeling.

It was a great gesture by the Indy Car organisers and by Carl to fix it so that I was able to run Red Five. According to the regulations, drivers are assigned numbers as a result of how they finished in the previous year's championship. On that basis, Bobby Rahal, the defending PPG Cup champion, started out the '93 season as Number One and Newman-Haas Racing should have taken numbers two and six to reflect the fact Michael Andretti finished second in the standings and Mario sixth. But Carl knew the Red Five was important to me and therefore tried to fix it so that we could get the number.

I thank Carl for doing that – and also Derrick Walker and his driver Scott

Left Phoenix International Raceway—an oasis in the desert. My first taste of the one-mile oval in competition was unfortunately brief . . . and painful.

Goodyear for agreeing to switch from Number Five, which they earned from the year before, to Number Two. The way it's worked out, everybody's happy, and the Indy Car organizers still have the continuity of numbering which is important in terms of marketing and overall acceptance of the series. It's yet another example of how everyone cooperates, works together, to ensure a harmony in Indy Car racing, possibly the single greatest difference between it and Formula 1.

Right Being able to maintain my links with 'Red Five' means a lot to me.

The Indianapolis 500

*I*ndy Car racing and specifically the Indianapolis 500 has an aura, a mystique all of its own. I can remember, as a child, sitting at home and watching the race on television. I thought then what an incredible event it was – although I must confess the thing that stuck in my mind most of all was how many accidents there were! Even so, Indianapolis has always been something I've wanted to do.

I think if you're a pure racer – and I like to consider myself a pure racer – then the biggest race in the world, period, is the Indianapolis 500. There's no question about it. The media coverage it commands is amazing. The track itself, the 2.5-mile super-speedway, is unlike any other. And the fact it draws almost half a million spectators on raceday makes it nothing less than a phenomenon. You just cannot compare it to any other single-day sporting event in the world. Not even in Formula 1. I believe the largest crowd a Formula 1 race ever attracted was around 300,000 one year at Monza, when Ferrari was winning the championship.

The Indianapolis Motor Speedway has been a crowd-puller ever since it was built in 1909. Several events were held during 1910, following pavement of the original crushed stone and tar surface with bricks, but after noting that attendances had dropped off, Carl Fisher made another inspired decision: to concentrate on one major event each year to be run over 500 miles and held on May 30, the traditional Memorial Day holiday taken in honour of those killed in the US Civil War of 1861–5.

A huge (for the times) $27,550 purse was posted for the inaugural 500-mile event in 1911, and 40 cars started the race. Most were entered by official factory teams. Starting positions were determined according to the order in which entries were received in the mail. A huge crowd was on hand, and Fisher added to the spectacle by introducing a new starting procedure. Instead of the cars accelerating away from a stand-still in the accepted fashion, Fisher the salesman himself led the field around for one parade lap in a Stoddard Dayton production car, affording everyone a slow-motion view of all the contestants. Then he pulled off to the side and signalled the race to begin.

Breathtaking view of the start of the Indianapolis 500. The unique scoring tower displays positions during the race, starting with the qualifying order. The pit lane is to the right. John Townsend's zoom lens foreshortens the front straight, but believe it or not the exit of Turn Four in the distance—you can just pick out the 'groove' of rubber arcing towards the wall—is almost three-quarters of a mile away!

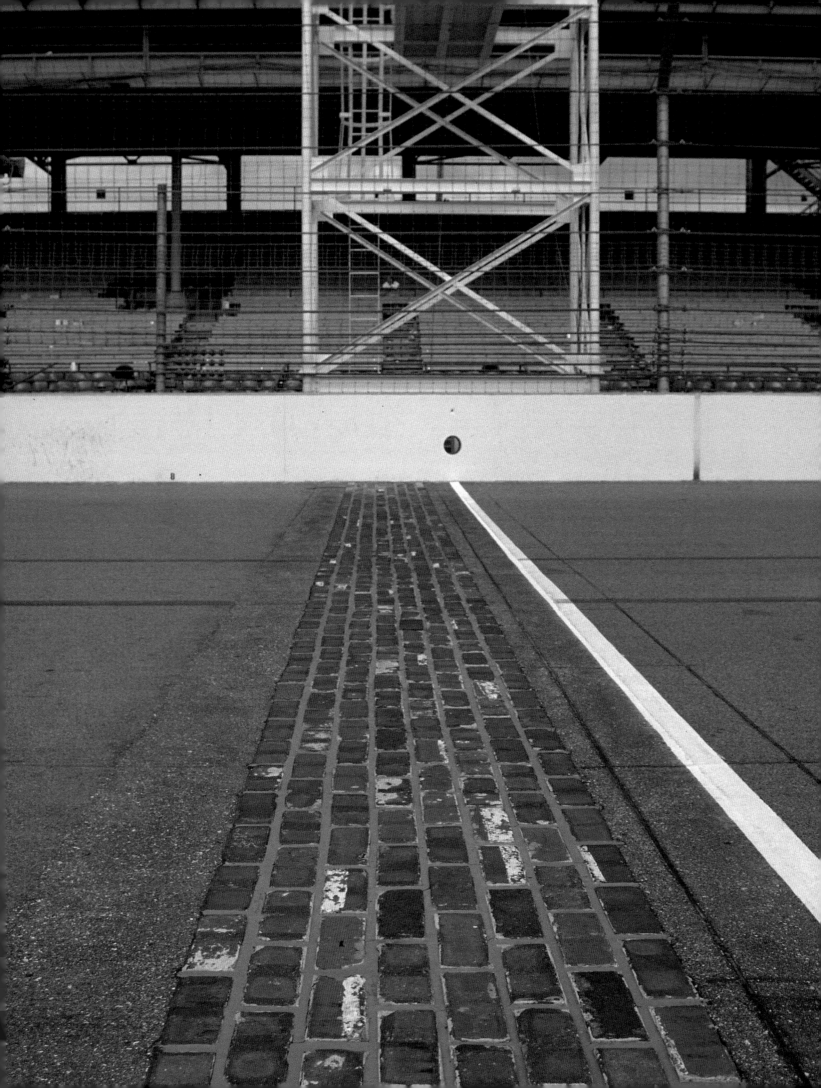

All bar one of the cars were two-seaters with a riding mechanic on board whose job it was to fix any problems that might arise and also keep an eye open for other, faster cars coming up behind. The exception was the six-cylinder high-tailed Marmon 'Wasp' of Ray Harroun. The Pennsylvania-born Marmon factory development engineer circulated at a consistent pace, anxious to minimize tyre wear. He was also alone, observing any approaching traffic by means of an ingenious reflective device mounted above the dashboard. Thus was born the rear-view mirror.

The race was a gruelling test of endurance for both car and driver. Harroun sought relief for a few laps from colleague Cyrus Patschke, then took the lead on lap 182 and went on to score a famous victory. Officially, at least. Second-place finisher Ralph Mulford vehemently disagreed, however, claiming he had won the race in his massive, almost 9-litre four-cylinder Lozier.

The controversy stemmed from an accident right in front of the scoring stand. With cars going hither and thither, some of the volunteer scorers apparently bolted and it was several laps before order could be restored. Mulford remained convinced he actually completed one more lap than he was given credit for. His protests fell on deaf ears. Harroun it was who took home the spoils.

In 1912 the cars were required to qualify one at a time, while in 1913 starting positions were determined according to a draw the night before the race. Frenchman Jules Goux became the first overseas winner that year, romping to victory in his revolutionary Grand Prix Peugeot. According to legend, Goux drew sustenance by gulping down a goodly quantity of his homeland's champagne during each pit stop. Despite that – or perhaps because of it – no one else even was close. Goux's eventual margin of victory was a huge 13 minutes and eight seconds, the widest in the history of the event. In those days all cars still running were allowed to complete the full 500 miles.

Goux's Peugeot, incidentally, was powered by a huge 7.6-litre engine which employed, for the first time, twin overhead camshafts, four valves per cylinder and monobloc castings. Today, of course, such features are commonplace; but not so in 1913.

European cars continued to dominate for the next few years. Rene Thomas won in 1914 for Frenchman Louis Delage. Howdy Wilcox was the fastest qualifier in 1915 with his locally built Stutz, earning the pole for the first time as starting positions were determined by speed, but Ralph de Palma (Mercedes) and Dario Resta (Peugeot) dominated the race. De Palma suffered a serious engine problem with less than three laps remaining, just as he had in 1912 when he led for 196 laps before retiring; this time he was able to limp home to a deserved victory.

'The Brickyard' is so named because 3.2 million bricks were used to 'pave' the circuit after its original surface of crushed stone and tar broke up disastrously in 1909. Over time, the entire 2.5-mile length has been re-covered with asphalt, although for the sake of tradition one yard of bricks is retained at the start/finish line.

The 1916 race was notable for several reasons. It drew the slimmest field in the event's fabled history, only 21 cars, and the smallest crowd. The Great War had taken its toll, in deference to which the organizers cut the race distance to 300 miles. It remains the one and only time the race has been scheduled for less than 500 miles, although on several occasions since it has been cut short due to inclement weather. The race track lay dormant in 1917 and 1918, used instead as an aviation repair depot, while 100 acres of land were farmed to help cover the costs of taxes and maintenance.

Racing resumed in 1919, whereupon Rene Thomas returned '*pour la gloire de la France*' and was the first to circulate at better than 100 mph in one of Ernest Ballot's latest creations. The Ballot was fearsomely fast, using a 4.9-litre engine designed by the Swiss engineer Ernest Henry who was also among the design team on the 1912 Peugeot. Unfortunately, it wasn't terribly reliable. Victory went to Wilcox's earlier Peugeot.

Sadly, two drivers and a riding mechanic were killed that same year, and at least in part because of that the regulations were changed for 1920 to allow a maximum engine size of only 183 cubic inches (3.0 litres). Four-lap qualifying runs were instituted for the first time.

The new rules fostered a growing trend towards American-built pure-bred racing engines, with the Duesenberg brothers, Fred and Augie, Louis Chevrolet and Harry Miller all emerging to design competitive powerplants in the early 1920s. Chevrolet's Frontenac, built in Indianapolis, broke the European stranglehold in 1920, driven by his brother Gaston. It wasn't until 19 years later that the Americans next relinquished victory in the world's most prestigious motor race.

More engine restrictions followed in 1923 (down to 122 cubic inches/2.0 litres) and again in 1926 (to 91 cubic inches, or a little under 1500 cc), whereupon Miller's incredible supercharged in-line eight-cylinder engine became virtually invincible. There were other changes, too. Carl Fisher began to devote more of his time to developing property in Miami Beach, Florida. Finally, in 1927, he and James Allison sold their majority share in the Speedway to former racer and World War I fighter 'ace' Eddie Rickenbacker.

Rather more distressing was the rising cost of racing. Expenditure, of course, is relative. Nowadays many Indy Car team owners are experiencing similar worries. A new Lola chassis is priced in excess of $400,000. Engines, which can only be leased, not bought, will set you back at least $1.25 million per car per season. By current Formula 1 standards, that is peanuts. A typical Formula 1 budget is in the scores of millions. For Indy Car teams, a budget of between seven and ten million dollars is enough to mount a top-line challenge.

In the late 1920s, the ubiquitous exquisitely built front-wheel drive Miller 91s were extremely expensive at more than $15,000 apiece. Some of the leading entrants at Indianapolis were spending in excess of $50,000 during the month of May alone. When you bear in mind a reasonable annual working wage in those days was somewhere around $1400, you can appreciate the extent of the concern.

Then came 'The Crash' of 1929 – not at Indianapolis, for a change, but on the Wall Street stock market. Rickenbacker was disturbed about the potential loss of entrants. He was mindful, too, that increasing specialization had frightened away the major manufacturers. So for 1930 he persuaded the AAA to adopt a new formula aimed at drastically reducing costs and attracting more passenger car suppliers back into the sport. Rickenbacker's plan succeeded in drawing such household names as Studebaker, Hudson, Buick and Ford to Indianapolis.

In 1933, an all-time record of forty-two cars started the race, although a stringent cutback on the prize fund, reduced to $54,450 from $93,900 the previous year, was partially responsible for a brief drivers' strike before the

Above George Bailey smiles proudly from the seat of his 1939 Gulf-Miller. The car was way ahead of its time, featuring a mid-engine layout, pannier fuel tanks, four-wheel drive and disc brakes on all four wheels. It

was also an expensive failure. Sadly, Bailey lost his life in an accident with the car the following year at Indy. *Below* An evocative sign above the entrance to the modern garage area at Indianapolis.

start. Sanity eventually prevailed, but only to a point, since what amounted to a demolition derby ended with five fatalities by the end of the month. The following year, the AAA restricted the number of starters to the now traditional 33. That same year, cars were required to complete 10-lap qualifying runs at an average speed in excess of 100 mph. The concept was continued until 1939, when the present regime of four-lap runs, first introduced in 1920, was recommenced.

Money, of course, was tight in the 1930s and Rickenbacker was spending an increasing proportion of his time and money on a more profitable enterprise, Eastern Air Lines. The deteriorating track surface brought an unacceptable number of serious injuries and fatalities during that era, and finally Rickenbacker was compelled to begin a wholesale improvement of the aging speedway. It started in 1935 with the construction of a new concrete retaining wall around the racing surface, and continued a year later with a widening of the turns. In 1937 the corners were paved with asphalt for the first time, followed in 1938 by the 'short chutes.'

By 1940 all bar the middle portion of the front straight, which retained its brick façade through entirely sentimental reasons, had been repaved. The infield run-off area had been enlarged, creating improved safety for spectators. But then came World War II. The Indianapolis Motor Speedway lay neglected and in disarray. When Wilbur Shaw, who had won at Indianapolis three times in the immediate pre-war period, ventured back to the track in the winter of 1944–5 to conduct some tyre testing on behalf of Firestone, he was appalled by what he found. Rickenbacker was in no position to fund the necessary renovation but he instructed Shaw to seek a suitable benefactor who would be willing to purchase the race track for the same price he had paid for it almost twenty years earlier – around $700,000.

After several months of searching, Shaw was introduced by investment and business broker Homer Cochran to wealthy Indiana businessman Anton 'Tony' Hulman Jr. He had no background in motor racing other than as a spectator but was an accomplished athlete. He was blessed also with an astute commercial mind and a keen perception of tradition and honour. His family had earned its fortune in the state of Indiana and the Indianapolis 500 represented a magical link between Indiana and the outside world. It provided a huge source of income and pride.

Hulman soon forged a deal with Rickenbacker whereby he would take over control of the property and Shaw would administer the race track on a day-to-day basis. The paperwork was concluded in November 1945. Shaw then set about the mammoth task of returning the neglected edifice of speed to its former glory. Rickenbacker, meanwhile, retained a close interest in the sport as chairman of the AAA Contest Board.

The old garage area, commonly known as 'Gasoline Alley', which had been badly damaged in a fire on the morning of the race in 1941, was rebuilt. Before too long all of the old decrepit wood grandstands had been replaced by new structures built of concrete and steel.

The improvements continued over the years. In 1956, when USAC took over the race sanction from the AAA, a new office and a museum was built on the corner of 16th Street and Georgetown Road, right outside the Turn One area. A year later the distinctive old timing-and-scoring pagoda, which was first erected opposite the start/finish line in 1913, then rebuilt in 1926 following a fire, was replaced, controversially, by a more modern control tower. In 1959 the unique electronic scoring tower appeared on the front straight. And finally, in 1961, all but one yard of brick at the start/finish line was paved over. Despite that, the historic circuit's 'Brickyard' moniker has remained to this day.

Hulman's guidance and Shaw's practicality saw the Indianapolis 500 continue to thrive in the post-war years. A record prize fund in excess of $115,000 was posted the first year; by 1948 that had grown to over $170,000. A year later Bill Holland became the first winner to take home more than $50,000.

Even as the race gained in stature, however, it became more insular than ever, with minimal overseas participation. From its very earliest days the Indianapolis 500 had attracted a significant influx of European drivers. Some of them raced in America at the behest of manufacturers who quickly came to envisage the benefits to be gained from a vast new marketplace; others were drawn by the riches on offer at Indy itself. Precious few stayed on to contest other races in the national championship season. It was Indianapolis or nothing.

In the 1950s the race duly was acknowledged by the world governing body, the Federation Internationale de l'Automobile (FIA), for what it was – the biggest motor racing event of all. It was included as a round of the World Drivers Championship; but it failed to draw more than token interest from across the Atlantic. The race was simply an anomalistic diversion for the Grand Prix teams.

The Indianapolis 500 continued to be the domain of American cars and drivers long after the FIA realized the futility of according it world championship status. Yet the undoubted lure remained. The prize money was immense by European standards. In 1957, Sam Hanks took home first-prize money of $103,844 from a total purse exceeding $300,000. It was more than the vast majority of his contemporaries earned in a lifetime.

The rest of the world began to sit up and take a renewed interest. In 1961, marking the 50th anniversary of the very first '500', Australian Jack Brabham started a veritable revolution at Indy – the 'rear-engine revolution' – with the tiny Cooper-Climax. Brabham, the winner of consecutive world championships in 1959 and 1960 with the British-built Coopers, caught on to the fact the relatively advanced suspension of his Formula 1 car was streets ahead of the technology employed by the Americans' front-engined Roadsters. The Cooper's nimble handling put the big bangers to shame in the corners. It was also far more economical on fuel and tyre wear.

My old friend, the late, great Colin Chapman was among the first to capitalize on the example set by Cooper and Brabham. The potential was obvious, especially to someone of Chapman's intuitive brilliance. Chapman and his driving star Jimmy Clark finally swept all before them at the third time of asking in 1965. Clark became the first overseas driver to win the great race since Resta, fifty years earlier. The British invasion also comprised cars built by Brabham, who returned with his own car in 1964 after splitting from the Cooper factory at the end of the 1961 season to establish his own racing car manufacturing business, and BRP (British Racing Partnership). Lola joined the band-wagon in 1965, and the following year was rewarded

Ford-powered Lotuses were the class of the field in 1965. Here Jimmy Clark heads to victory in his factory car, chased by A. J. Foyt and Parnelli Jones. Top finishing Rookie that year was my current teammate Mario Andretti, who finished third.

Right Arie Luyendyk, despite his background in road racing, has developed into something of a specialist on the ovals.

with a victory by Graham Hill, whose son Damon is now winning in Formula 1 having taken over my place in the Williams-Renault team.

In the 1980s, several drivers gave up promising careers in Europe in order to try and make a name for themselves in North America. Their sights were set squarely on the Indianapolis 500. Among them was Geoff Brabham – Sir Jack's eldest son – and Dutchman Arie Luyendyk. Both were very successful. Geoff won championships in Formula Super Vee and Can-Am before graduating onto the Indy Car circuit. He was very competitive once again, although he never seemed to have much luck on his side and eventually was forced to quit due to a lack of sponsorship. Instead he took a factory drive with Nissan in the International Motor Sports Association's (IMSA) Camel GTP sports car championship. Geoff dominated that scene and won four straight titles. Now he's trying to get back onto the Indy Car circuit.

Luyendyk, another talented contemporary of mine from the Formula 3 days, pursued the same route. He, too, won a Super Vee crown and was finally rewarded with a victory at Indianapolis in 1990. He almost won in 1993 as well. Colombian-born Roberto Guerrero was another. He followed me through the ranks of British national championship racing, from Formula Ford to Formula 3, Formula 2 and up into Grand Prix racing. Roberto, like so many others, never quite got the break he deserved. I was lucky. I was picked up by Colin Chapman at Lotus. Roberto struggled away with a couple of lesser teams in Formula 1, always bringing sponsorship, before he got smart. He realized he could earn a better living in North America. He hooked up quickly with a very good, well-sponsored team run by legendary Indy Car chief mechanic George Bignotti, and in 1984 almost won Indianapolis at his first attempt. Roberto is still a force to be reckoned with on the PPG Cup scene.

In 1983, Italian Teo Fabi, another talented driver who had come up through the European ranks, surprised everyone at Indy by qualifying his British-built March on the pole. Irishman Derek Daly moved to the States after driving in Formula 1 for Ensign, March, Tyrrell and, like me, Williams. Derek has retired from driving now but he's still involved as a commentator for ESPN television.

The European accent remains very much a part of the Indianapolis scene. As soon as you arrive at the hallowed Speedway, however, it becomes obvious there is nothing like it in Europe. This is no ordinary racing circuit. It is utterly unique.

Before I went there for the first time I tried to keep an open mind about the place. I'd heard all sorts of stories, of course, some good and some bad, but I wanted to judge it for myself. I tried to go there without any pre-conceived ideas. And believe me that's not very easy, because even from the air at 5000 feet, flying into a small airport about five miles away, you can see The Speedway, large as life. To use the American vernacular, it's a very awesome place indeed. It's very, very different. Stupefying. Stunning. Steeped in history.

It has a distinctive atmosphere. I was aware of it as soon as I drove underneath the tunnel and went into the infield by the museum. It's amazing. You can't help but notice the amount of concrete. It's daunting. One thing struck me right away: that you do not want to make a mistake at Indy – or if you do, you want to make it very small.

I'd compare my arrival at Indianapolis with when I was driving for Ferrari in Formula 1 and I went to the factory at Maranello for the first time. I met some people who'd been working there for fifty years, and there's no question there was a special atmosphere, a charisma about the whole place. Indianapolis was the same.

Later when I ventured out onto the circuit it gave me a feeling only a driver can understand. It was incredible. Going across the strip of bricks at the start/finish line was a very special sensation. Eerie almost. Especially when I think back on the event's history. I'm also glad the bricks are only a yard wide, because they give you quite a jolt inside the car!

The Indianapolis Motor Speedway really is a special place. It's been listed on the National Register of Historic Places since 1975. It was recognized as a National Historic Landmark in 1987. Rightly so. The Hulman family has done an incredible job in developing the circuit over the years. There is a new 18-hole golf course being built this year, designed by one of the world's most renowned golf course architects, Pete Dye. It replaces the original one built back in 1929. There is the Speedway Motel situated on the outside of

Above Roberto Guerrero resurrected his career by switching to the Indy Car scene and finishing second at Indy on his debut.
Below Teo Fabi was a Rookie sensation in 1983, winning four races and taking the pole at Indy.

Above Turn One, lap one at Indy. I'm already tucked down to the inside, following Al Unser Jr., Scott Goodyear, Stefan Johansson (16), Emerson Fittipaldi and Paul Tracy. But bear in mind we're already travelling at close to 200 mph.

Turn Two, which this year celebrates its 30th anniversary. The Hall of Fame Museum, opened along with new offices in 1976, is a must-see. The huge double-tier grandstand which stretches almost the length of the front straight is imposing. In recent years the track has added extra grandstand seating, more and more hospitality suites and a new garage area, which is extremely functional, although I must say rather featureless.

'Tony' Hulman Jr. continued to preside over The Speedway in a benevolent manner until his death, aged 76, in 1977. Earlier that same year, following the first total repaving of the track since the bricks were laid in 1909, A. J. Foyt, a name equally synonymous with Indianapolis, won for a record fourth time. Afterwards Mr Hulman accompanied Foyt on his lap of honour. It must have been a poignant moment.

The Hulman family has been in charge of proceedings at Indianapolis continuously since the war. Tony's grandson, Tony George, now presides over the world-class facility. This past year he was responsible for some of the most significant alterations ever made. The changes included a completely new perimeter wall, both taller and stronger than its predecessor, which had stood since the 1930s, and provision of a new 'warm-up' lane inside the racing surface itself. The 'racing line', the optimum line through the corner, is now appreciably different than it used to be.

Some people have asked whether those changes made it a little easier for me, because everyone else had to find their way around, learn the new line, but really I don't think it helped me at all. The more miles you do on a circuit, the better.

Above The imposing façade to the Speedway Hall of Fame Museum and main offices at the 'Racing Capital of the World'.

I agree with the changes they've made. What they've effectively done is make the track narrower than before. Speeds are significantly reduced. Where now the inside of the corner is defined by a white line, a section of corrugated asphalt, called a 'rumble strip', and then a 12-feet strip of grass, there used to be just a wide-open 'apron' of asphalt which gave the opportunity for drivers to cut inside the old white line and effectively shorten the corner.

Some of the drivers who'd been going to Indianapolis for years, including my teammate Mario, had a hard time adapting to the new line that's required, but that didn't make it any easier for me. I still had to try to go round the corner as quick, or quicker, than everyone else. It's still tough.

Another thing I noticed as soon as I got to Indianapolis was the professionalism of everybody there. I had no knowledge of what I was letting myself in for, no comfort zone; but lots of people came forward to help. I think the best advice came from A. J. Foyt. 'Don't turn right, boy,' he said in that broad Texan drawl of his, 'or you'll eat concrete!' I've already done that, thank you, I replied. At Phoenix. It's not something I wanted to repeat. A.J.'s fantastic. He's wonderful. I spent some time with him before the beginning of the season in Phoenix, filming a commercial for Texaco. I've never had so much fun doing a commercial in my life.

Mario was a big help too. He helped me avoid some of the pitfalls that you go through as a 'Rookie', as all the first-year drivers are called. And everyone at The Speedway, and USAC, were so helpful. Each year before the race they have what's known as the Rookie Orientation Programme. It actually takes place on the weekend before the track first opens for practice –

Right The ultimate status symbol at Indianapolis: the Borg-Warner Trophy which features the names and a likeness of all the winners in bas-relief.

which is almost a month before the race itself.

The agenda starts off with a session in the classroom where they talk about the track, about the importance of warming up the car, building up your confidence and generally making it crystal clear that patience is a vital virtue. They go through all the procedures, talk about traffic and the lines you'll need to take as you get up speed.

They spend a whole day going over everything there is to know about Indianapolis before anyone gets to go out on the circuit. Once onto the track, the officials are very meticulous about making the rookies build up their speed gradually, so they have an opportunity to get used to the high velocities. If you think about it, when something happens at 220 mph, it tends to happen extremely quickly!

How the on-track portion of the rookie programme works is that the driver has to complete 10-lap 'phases' at incrementally faster speeds. You have to start off with 10 laps at under 180 mph, then complete another 10 laps between 180 and 185, 185 and 190, 190 and 195, and 195 and 200. The final phase is to run 10 consecutive laps above 200 mph. Through each segment the drivers are observed by seasoned professionals who will make comments according to your line through the corners, your consistency, or whatever. Assuming you get through all that during the rookie-only weekend, all that remains is to be 'observed' for a final 10-lap run by some veteran drivers while other cars are on the track. That takes place once official practice has begun.

The whole programme is a great idea. Essential. I don't care who you are. To get up to speed slowly is very, very important. There are some big steps involved. The programme gives the driver a chance to acclimatize himself and it gives the officials a chance to say yes, he's up to speed. The importance cannot be underestimated because it's not just a case of you hurting yourself out there; one mistake and you can hurt someone else. Very seriously indeed. We're talking about the potential of killing somebody. So when you bring it down to the seriousness of the beast, which is very serious indeed, I think what USAC does is very, very professional.

Unfortunately, I didn't get the chance to take advantage of this luxury. Instead I had been at home in Florida, recuperating from the effect of an operation on my back, a legacy of my crash at Phoenix. I didn't arrive at Indy until midway through the first week of official practice and by that time everyone was already up to speed and working on their qualifying setups.

I have to say that USAC and Tony George were fantastic in allowing me to delay taking my 'Rookie Test' until I got there. They didn't have to do that, and obviously if they hadn't accommodated me in the way they did, it would have been impossible for me to take part. I owe a big thank you to Tony George and the USAC officials, and also to Dr Terry Trammell, Indy Car racing's resident medical expert, and my specialist physician from Florida, Dr George Morris. They made the whole thing possible and they allowed me to do my Rookie Test out of sequence with everyone else.

In some ways it was tougher for me to go through the procedures when I did because I didn't have the benefit of a clear track. I had to worry about all the yellow flags and all sorts of other people on the track. There were people whistling past me left, right and centre for the first few laps. It was

Terry Trammell (*right*), one of the many specialists and surgeons of the Indy Car circuit. With him and his team at every race, all drivers feel a little safer.

a hair-raising experience.

It was very different and it was very difficult because I had cars going round my ears at 220 mph, and to start off with I was only allowed to do 180. So I had to stay off the racing line, get round the corners and still do 180 and be within a band of 5 mph for the first 10-lap phase.

I was very lucky. My mechanics and my engineer Peter Gibbons did a fantastic job in my absence, and also I need to thank Mario Andretti for running some laps in my race car and my T-car, the spare car, to make sure everything was OK. That was very gracious of him and I think it says a lot about the sort of man he is. The team was magnanimous in its support. Not only at the race circuits but when I was away and hurting and sore, they constantly kept in contact, always motivating me and keeping me informed with what was going on. My comfort zone was helped enormously by knowing I was probably in the best hands I could possibly be in – and I'm talking about not only the management of the team, the owners, but everyone involved in the entire operation.

It really helped that the team was up to speed, so to speak, with the car. They gave me good data and all I had to do was tune the car to the way I like to drive. I'm not saying that's easy, because it isn't, but having the Newman-Haas team behind me was an enormous help.

When I went out onto the track I just wanted to get the Rookie Test over with as efficiently and as quickly as possible. It was quite difficult at times because the yellow lights kept coming on so that track inspections could be made but again USAC was very gracious because if I ran two laps and then a yellow came on, those two laps counted towards the 10 – as long as they were within the speed zone that was required.

The Rookie Test went quite well. I went out with a full tank of fuel to start with and was able to get through the first three phases all in one run. We were very fortunate to do that. Then we topped off the fuel and despite a few 'yellow' interruptions we just had to do one more 10-lap run at over 200 with the observers in place.

A.J. was one of those entrusted with watching my progress in the final part of the Rookie Test and afterwards he came up to me and said, 'You sonofabitch' (which I think means 'splendid fellow' in Texas), 'do you realize it's been 10 years since I went out and observed? You owe me,' he went on, 'because somebody out there tried to kill me!' Apparently there was a big accident on the corner where he was standing, Turn One, and he was almost hit by a chunk of debris. He was 'very expressive', let's say! It was very amusing for me, although I guess he wasn't quite so impressed. If you haven't gathered, I like A.J. a lot.

That apart, we got the Rookie Test out of the way fairly easily and comfortably. Looking back I'm very glad I had to go through it. I think it's an excellent system and it doesn't matter whether you're a world champion or not; the way the USAC officials run it is first-class. It certainly helped me and I respected it and I enjoyed doing it. I learned a lot before I went out there to try and set some quick times.

Once I'd got the Test out of the way, I decided to try and go a little bit quicker. We got up to 218.579 mph, which was 10th quickest of the day at the time. I was quite pleased with that.

Then I had a rest!

Below A great legend and character in Indy Car racing and the first four-time winner at Indianapolis, A. J. Foyt wears a broad smile after announcing his retirement this past May.

We all went back to the garage and thought about it a little bit. We changed one very small thing on the car – not very much at all – and then I had a fresh set of tyres and we were able to do just a couple of laps, a 221.7 I think it was and a 222.855, before we called it a day. We figured we'd done enough on the first day.

Of course, I was delighted. But it wasn't easy. There were several barriers to overcome. You can probably get up to 200 mph without too much difficulty, but 205, 210, 215 and anything over 215, then you've got to start stretching yourself big-time.

I think every driver probably has his own personal barrier. The personal barrier is how late you can keep your foot on the accelerator as you go into the corner and how soon you can get it back on again. It's tough. My personal barrier was 220, 222–224 and 224–226. You just have to work at it. You work hard. It's enlightening. It's very tricky. It's very daunting. It's very, very uncomfortable – especially if the wind is blowing a bit and you have to commit to going into these corners and not be sure you have enough room on the exit. That always catches a few people out. One time the car moved about six feet, but fortunately I'd left a margin of about six-feet-one, so I was alright. But it was close. Again, it helps teach you: you just have to build up slowly.

The biggest thing to concentrate on at Indianapolis is paying attention – paying very serious attention! A couple of times I came up on some slower cars going into Turns Three and Four and I got into what the drivers call 'dirty air'. That's when the turbulence from the cars in front takes away downforce from your front wings and destabilizes your car. It's not very comfortable. You have to get out of the throttle and be careful not to slide too close to the wall.

I certainly learned a lot of lessons about a super-speedway. I have the utmost respect for it and I have the utmost admiration for the officials and the way they conduct everything about Indianapolis. It's so professional. If there's any doubt whatsoever, if someone thinks they see a small piece of debris or perhaps a hot dog wrapper or oil or fluid or anything, the yellow lights go on. When that happens, everyone has to slow down and go back to the pits. It can be quite frustrating as a driver, especially if you haven't seen anything and you're on a good lap. It's the same feeling when you go out for just one lap and the yellows come back on again. That seems to happen quite a lot. But you have to remember that the yellows, the cautions, are for your safety and your well-being. They add to your comfort zone.

I was able to programme myself to accept the yellows. It was processed into my mind as I knew it was for my own security. The officials' pro-fessionalism is exemplary. And when you get back in the car and go out onto the track, you know it's clean. That's a reassuring thing, especially at the speeds we're doing. They certainly gave me a lot of confidence. Believe it or not, being so uncomfortable in the car due to the injury to my back may have given me the patience to cope with the yellows and the interruptions. I was very pleased with the way I handled that. I was on a hot lap a couple of times when the yellows came out but I just kept saying to myself, 'Look what happened to Nelson...'.

For anyone who's unaware, Nelson Piquet, a three-time world champion, had a terrible crash at Indianapolis last year. He hadn't been to Indianapolis

In conference with Peter Gibbons about car handling.

before. He was fast right away but he got impatient as a result of all the interruptions, the cautions. He ended up in hospital with two very badly broken legs. He was a mess. When I thought about that, it acted as a good wake-up call.

Talking of Nelson, he came in for a lot of criticism this year for coming back after everything that he went through. What it boils down to is that everybody does the race for their own reasons. My reason for doing it is because I signed a contract for twelve months. I've got no idea why Nelson decided to do it, just the one race, when he hadn't driven for so many months, that's a question only he can answer. All I would say is that given all the experience he has and his accomplishments, a lot of people were very surprised. It's very difficult to go to Indy and be competitive without having a thorough knowledge of your car, and I don't see how anyone could gain the necessary experience from driving it at Indy alone.

Having said that, Indianapolis seems to have a hold on some people. It's like a drug. It has incredible drawing power. I think if you've been indoctrinated with Indy early enough, it does that to you. It's a fantastic race and it's built up to be the biggest race in the world – which it is. It carries a lot of weight in America especially, and if you win at Indianapolis then your future in racing is secure.

The real keys to Indianapolis are experience and motivation. Some of the drivers that come back year after year, like Al Unser senior and Jim Crawford and Stan Fox, these people are highly motivated. The actual physical effort at Indy is different to that required on a road circuit. But the technical effort and expertise is immense and therefore they can apply all their expertise; and even if they are getting a little bit older, it doesn't slow them down at Indy. Because physically the Super-Speedway races are not very demanding at all – nothing like as tough as the road races or the shorter ovals.

On the other hand there are some very accomplished road racers who have driven briefly at Indianapolis and hated it. I think I understand why. Firstly, they probably weren't competitive – that always influences your feelings – and if you're not competitive you're not going to sing praises about the place. The reason they weren't competitive was probably because they didn't have the right team or the right equipment – so they frightened themselves. And believe me, it's very easy to frighten yourself with the right equipment, let alone the wrong equipment! I can totally understand their feelings and I wouldn't disagree because people's feelings are their own. They're very strong emotions and you can't pooh-pooh them; you must listen to them. No matter who you are, it's important to listen.

There's no question, the way the car is set up and the experience of the team are vitally important. It's true at any race track but particularly on a super-speedway. Again, and I can't emphasize this enough, that's why I've been so fortunate. My team was protecting me because of the accident I had in Phoenix. They know what to change on the car and what effect those changes are likely to have, and so whenever I asked for more front wing, for example, they were really reluctant to do anything. Trimming the car on the rear, by which I mean lessening the wing angle slightly to give a little less downforce and therefore aerodynamic drag, they were really reluctant again. I almost had to prove to them that what I was saying about the car, about how it was reacting, was true.

Car setup is absolutely critical for the high speed ovals. The front wings are covered up, but even so it's noticeable how much smaller the wings are than for a road course or a short oval.

Now I don't disagree with that, because what happened in Phoenix was the result of a joint mistake by myself and the team. We made too much of an alteration on the car. We changed something too much. And we got bitten. With hindsight we didn't need to make that change, and in any case if we made that change again, we'd do something else at the same time to ensure we would maintain the car's balance. So you learn. The more things you try, the more you learn. The team is no different from me. They learn new things every day, the same as I do.

As I gained more experience at Indy, ran more laps, I was able to get a better feel. Closer and closer to raceday I started to change the car, make suggestions of my own which my engineer agreed with. By raceday our car was different to Mario's. Some of the changes were very significant.

Car set-up, as I've said, is crucial at Indianapolis. There are so many things you can do to the car, so many minute changes. It's tough to decide what might provide the best combination. And what makes the decision process even more difficult is the fact that track conditions can change hour by hour, day by day. The car is incredibly susceptible to changes in the weather conditions. Wind, air temperature, air density – whether there's humidity in the air, or it's dry – sunshine, cloud cover, these can all affect the race track and alter the performance of the car by something like 5 or 6 mph per lap.

That's one of the reasons why there's so much practice time at Indianapolis. It's totally unlike any other race track. For all of the other races there will be two, sometimes only one day of practice and qualifying, followed by the race on Sunday. At Indy, though, there is a whole week of practice before the start of qualifying, which is held over two days. Then there's another five days of practice before the second weekend of qualifying.

With all the different conditions that are likely to prevail, you need maybe three or four different set-ups for the whole month – and sometimes radically different set-ups – in order to find the right combination for the prevailing conditions in qualifying. And then on raceday you've just got to guess and hope that you're somewhere near, because the car's handling will often will be totally different on full tanks, in race trim, in comparison to when you were running the car as light as possible for qualifying.

Likewise the procedures at Indianapolis bear no relation to the remainder of the IndyCar schedule. Take qualifying, for example. It's incredibly complicated. The first day of qualifying, the opening Saturday, is Pole Day. Only on that day is everyone eligible to snag the pole. As on the other ovals, you draw for your position in the qualifying order. Qualifying starts on the button at 11 am, at which point the first car in line has been through the rigorous scrutinizing inspection and is ready to roll out onto the track. Each driver has two warm-up laps before being shown the green flag at the start/finish line. You then have to do four laps, with the cumulative time of all four counting as your qualifying time and speed. You'll be shown a green flag as you flash under the gantry to start lap two, then a white flag the next time around which reminds you there's one lap to go. Next time past you'll be greeted by the chequered flag.

Then it's time to start breathing again!

If, however, your team decides the car hasn't fulfilled its full potential, the crew chief can signify that fact to the official starter and he will wave the yellow flag. That's called a 'wave-off'. It happened to me this year,

Everything is different at Indy. The drivers' briefing is held in the open air with all the qualifiers seated according to the grid order. It's my turn to be introduced to the surprisingly large crowd on the Tower Terrace, situated right in front of the pit area but behind the

camera. Pole winner Arie Luyendyk is seated at the bottom left. Indy Car racing now is almost as cosmopolitan as Formula 1. In 1981 there was only one foreign driver in the field of 33 starters. This year there were 15, including the top four finishers.

because on my first qualifying attempt we had a dodgy pop-off valve so the engine wasn't producing maximum horsepower. I was struggling to break 217 mph, when I'd lapped at better than 225 earlier in the week.

Each car is allowed to make three qualifying attempts. If the car doesn't make it into the field, for whatever reason, that's it. That particular car can take no further part in the proceedings. It's benched, as they say in America. That's why all the top teams will enter at least two cars for each driver.

Then if you crash a car or one of them isn't up to speed for some reason, you have at least one backup.

Everyone will routinely run both (or all if there's more than two) cars during practice to ensure both are on a par. The team owner will put both cars into the qualifying draw. That way, for example, if his cars are in contention for the pole and rain is forecast for later in the day and he's drawn one high number and one low number, he can send out one of the cars early on to go for the pole. Because if you don't qualify on the first day, for whatever reason, you won't be eligible for the pole. No matter how fast you run.

As one car completes its qualifying attempt, whether successfully or not, the next one in line is sent on its way. If you decide to pull out of the line, you have to go all the way to the back of the order. Then, but only if there's time before the 6 pm finishing gun goes off, you can have another go and still be able to contend for the pole. But it's a gamble. If time runs out you can be left high and dry.

Occasionally there may be a lull in qualifying during the middle of the afternoon. May at Indianapolis tends to be characterized by hot, humid weather, and in those conditions the cars are at their least effective. They lose grip and speed. The best times to make a qualifying run are early in the day or late in the evening, when the air is cooler and thinner and there's less aerodynamic drag. The cars are at their most efficient. The problem, however, is that you're at the mercy of the draw and the weather. There's not much you can do about either of those parameters.

Sometimes, if it's hot, someone, somewhere along the line may decline the option to go out on the track. If there's no one else behind willing to take the gamble and go, the status quo remains. At that stage the officials will open up the track for practice. Anyone is free to go out and perhaps test the water, so to speak, check up on how the car is handling in the prevailing conditions. Often it can be a real game of cat-and-mouse. Particularly when the grid is almost full. Then it's a question of who's going to take the plunge first and get back into the qualifying line. As soon as someone does, the track is closed, inspected and readied for the next qualifying attempt.

At the end of the first day of qualifying, the order at the 'sharp end' of the starting grid is set, with the fastest cars at the front, of course. A maximum of 33 cars are permitted to start the race, ranked in 11 rows of three.

The second day of qualifying, or Time Trials as they are more properly known, is used to determine the order farther down the field. All second-day qualifiers line up behind the first-day qualifiers, irrespective of speed. The same goes for anyone who qualifies on the third and fourth days – on the second weekend. Thus, while it's not inconceivable that someone might set the fastest time of all on the final day of qualifying, he nevertheless will have to start behind all those who qualified on each of the preceding days.

That explains how the grid is finalized. Except, you guessed, it's not quite as simple as that! Once the grid is full and 33 cars have qualified, then the 'bumping' begins. That's when things really start to get exciting. When that occurs, the qualifier with the slowest average speed is said to be 'on the bubble'. If anyone else comes along and sets a faster time, the guy 'on the

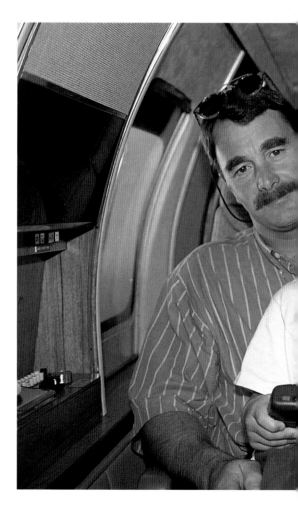

Overleaf The bands have marched and the anthems have been sung. Thousands of balloons are released into the clear Indiana sky. Now it's time for the real action as the crews prepare to fire up the engines. It's an incredible sight with more than 400,000 people cheering wildly.

Below En route to Indianapolis with Greg and Leo.

bubble' gets 'bumped' out of the field. Finally, when the gun goes off at 6 pm on the final day, the fastest 33 qualifiers will make up the field.

This year's qualifying was especially exciting. There was a fair amount of bumping on the last day and it all ended with Bobby Rahal, the defending PPG Cup champion and former Indianapolis 500 winner, going out right as the gun sounded in a frantic last-ditch attempt to make the field. If you can get out onto the track before the gun goes off, you're eligible to complete that run. Bobby had been struggling all month long to get up to the required speed and here he was with one final opportunity. He wasn't fast enough. He didn't make it. So he had to suffer the ignominy of not qualifying for the biggest race of all. It must have been a bitter pill to swallow. It was impossible not to feel sorry for him, especially after all the hard work that had gone into trying to develop his own car.

In case you hadn't realized, qualifying is a big deal at Indianapolis. Pole Day attracts a huge crowd. In fact I think it's the second biggest attendance draw in the entire sporting world – beaten only by the race itself.

If you're in contention for the pole, or even if you're not, there's a lot of pressure on the driver. The Speedway takes on a whole new feeling from the previous days of practice. The crowd is immense. Everyone cheers as each driver starts his run. You can hear it when you're in the car. The atmosphere's intense. And it's something you can't pre-judge. As far as driving the car is concerned, you have to make four perfect laps. One mistake and it's over.

I don't think it was as difficult for me as it was for the other rookie drivers. I'd watched it on videos and I'd been in situations like that before – at Silverstone and other places. I put myself in the same mode as getting ready for qualifying at the British Grand Prix. It wasn't a problem. Once again, I tried to keep a totally open mind, which I think was a strength. I tried to do that all month long. I paid special attention to my feelings and senses, my intuition, and I tried to listen well for the whole month. I think that contributed to a good result at the end of the day.

Once qualifying is over, then, finally, there's some time to relax. The cars don't run again until Thursday, which is Carburetion Day. The name goes back to earlier days when the crews would make final adjustments to their cars, and especially to the carburettor, in final preparation for the race. Of course, many years have passed since any car ran a carburetted engine at Indianapolis. Nowadays they all have electronic fuel injection. But that's just another example of the strength of tradition at Indianapolis.

As far as we were concerned, having qualified solidly on the first day, we made all of our preparation for the race while many of the drivers were still worried about whether or not they'd make it into the race. We did all our full-tank running, tyre checks and everything else during the week in between qualifying. Then I went home to Florida to relax a little, give my body a better opportunity to recuperate in time for the race.

Then I returned for Carburetion Day, just for a final check on the car. This was another new experience for me in a year of new experiences. It's extraordinary to have the 'warmup' three days before the race. We were very limited as to the number of laps I could run because of the endurance of the engine, so we used that session just to do a systems check. It was good, it was useful, because we found a few hiccups, a few things we needed

to take care of, but I would've liked to have done another 50 laps to get ready for the race.

The following day, Friday, brought another 'first', the customary rookie meeting. It was held in an office at the track and hosted by the veteran chief steward Tom Binford, his assistant Art Meyers and two of the more prominent drivers, in this case three-time winner Johnny Rutherford and four-time winner Al Unser. Between them they had well over a hundred years of experience at Indianapolis. They were well worth listening to. The meeting was very interesting and very helpful.

They brought up a lot of subjects that we needed to pay attention to. Most significantly, if we were running in a pack of cars and if someone at the front of the pack – maybe three or four or five cars in front of you – has a 'moment' and clips the wall, we wouldn't know about it until we were on top of it. It was a sobering thought. Again they stressed the importance of looking ahead, thinking ahead. If someone up ahead makes a mistake or has a problem, you have to pay very special attention because at 220 mph there's virtually no opportunity to take any avoiding action. Not at that speed. And especially with the 'narrower' track this year, which doesn't give you the benefit of using the old 'apron' as an escape route, so to speak.

So you have to programme that aspect into your game-plan. If you see cars backing up in front, don't just duck out and try to pass them because they're probably backing up for a very good reason which you can't see. It was a very good piece of advice. They also told us that whatever pre-conceived ideas we had from looking at videos or whatever, when Sunday morning comes along and the grandstands are full and the place is filled with people, the atmosphere conveys a whole new sensation. All of a sudden it seems to be a lot narrower. Because of all the people.

Johnny and Al hammered home the importance of being patient. They and other great drivers such as Rick Mears, another four-time winner, said that the race is won and lost over the last few pit stops. The majority of the race you have to work on the car, the balance of the car, make sure the tyres are alright, maintain a good pace, try to keep on the lead lap, and then it's down to the last five or ten laps whether you win or lose.

They turned out to be prophetic words.

I think the experiences I'd already had in 1993 helped me enormously. My training in patience has been absolutely phenomenal and I'm sure that helped me at Indy in a weird sort of way. I think I demonstrated a lot of patience during the month of May. We started late and we had to get up to speed and we didn't rush it, we just took our time. It worked out for us.

There was one funny instance where my patience was a little bit iffy. It was when I was leaving the track after Carburetion Day, in the evening, and I stopped at the traffic lights right outside the race track. I had the radio on and I was with some friends in the car and we heard this s-s-c-c-r-r-r … BANG! I looked at the car alongside me, just a couple of feet away, and it had been hit up the backside by another car which had in turn been hit by yet another car – at about 40 or 50 mph. It was a big accident. The three cars just became squashed together like a huge concertina. I was just looking and thinking … I'm glad I was in this lane!

It certainly provided a little diversion from all the rest of the action. That final week before the race encompasses all sorts of different functions.

Above Downtown Indianapolis draws a huge throng for the traditional pre-race parade on Saturday.

Right The parade is one of the myriad functions all the drivers attend in the build-up to the Indianapolis 500. The new Chevrolet Corvette was the pace car this year.

There are golf tournaments, tennis tournaments, fashion shows, parades, dinners, fêtes, you name it. It's quite incredible. And it's great, too, because they end up raising a heck of a lot of money for a whole host of different charities. They do a wonderful job.

It's all part of the big picture at Indianapolis. It's far more than just another motor race. The prize money at Indianapolis shows you that. The rewards are immense. They're huge. This year Tony George and his people paid out a record total purse of $7,681,300. The winner, Emerson Fittipaldi, earned $1,155,304, including all the various bonuses, although much of that, of course, is divided up among the team. It just shows how far the race has come.

At the same time, though, you have to try to treat Indianapolis like any other race. It's not like any other race but you have to approach it with the same attitude. In many ways it's the only race. It has an order of magnitude well above any other race or any other sporting event in the world. But you have to look at it from the same perspective as any other race. The winner takes home twenty PPG Cup championship points, just like every other race in the season.

Some drivers become overawed with it all and so they don't perform at their best. I tried to keep as low-key as possible. And next year, assuming I go back, I shall probably try to maintain an even lower profile than I did

Below Her Majesty the Queen gave a special dispensation to allow me to be featured on a special set of gold coins which are now legal tender on the Isle of Man. A special presentation was made during the month at Indianapolis by Donald Gelling, MHK.

INDIANAPOLIS

Above The amount of media interest generated at Indy is incredible. Here we are at one of the many press conferences.

this year. It's tough, because the pressure is immense. From everyone. From your team, from yourself and especially from the media. It's the biggest race in the world. It's bigger than Formula 1. It attracts an incredible volume of publicity. Everyone's thirsty because of Indianapolis.

I've been approached by a lot of the English and European press and a lot of other people I've never seen before from Japan, Australia and of course North America. I've done my best to accommodate everyone but I've had more demands on my time this year than I ever had in my Formula 1 career! It's been great, but I've had to ask all these people to try to remember I still have a job to do as well.

And at Indianapolis, that's no mean task. It's probably the toughest challenge I've ever come up against. It lived up to all my expectations – and more.

Indy Car Racing in 1993

Above I felt so proud and privileged to win my very first Indy Car race, especially in Australia because I've never won there before. Australia's almost like a home country to me. It's very similar to England in so many ways.

*B*y winning the Formula 1 World Championship in 1992 I achieved one of my boyhood dreams. This year, thanks to the opportunity presented to me by Carl Haas, Paul Newman and the various team sponsors, I have had a fresh new challenge, a chance to pursue what I classify as a 'world championship across the pond' – across the Atlantic in America. It is a challenge I relish.

It's been especially interesting for me because for a change I've been the underdog and there's so much I've had to learn. It's curious being referred to as a Rookie – a first-year driver – but that's exactly what I am. I've had my learner plates on, my rookie stripes.

On the open road in America you're not required to carry 'L' plates like we do in England, but I still had to apply for my driver's licence in Florida and for that I had to go through a short road test, just like I did at home all those years ago. It was very strange. In fact I had my Rookie Test at Indianapolis and my road test in Florida all in the same week. I don't think I've ever been as nervous as when I was taking my driver's test, because can you imagine what it would have been like if I'd failed? When I passed, I said to my instructor, you'll never even know how relieved I am!

I wasn't nervous when I went to Australia for the first round of the PPG Cup series, but neither was I totally sure what I was letting myself in for. The Surfers Paradise circuit was quite different to most of the other temporary circuits I'd driven on and I knew I had an awful lot to learn; but through being at one with the team and operating and functioning as a professional driver, that really wasn't a problem. I knew that my own personal comfort zone would improve as soon as I started getting races under my belt.

I was quite impressed with how the track was laid out. It had obviously been very well planned. The way the chicanes were laid out, with the curbing, then a strip of grass and the gravel trap, was far and away the best I've ever seen on a street circuit anywhere in the world. The chicanes were constructed so that if you did happen to nudge a curb it wasn't going to upset the car a lot. And obviously that's very, very important on a street circuit where you have to operate in extremely confined conditions.

Overleaf The crowd was phenomenal at Surfers Paradise and I was delighted to reward the fans with a win.

The track has two long straights where the cars reach almost 190 mph, but the run-off areas had also been properly planned. There were tyre barriers to help slow down any wayward cars, and the way the tyres had been put together and netted was very similar – or even better – than the way it's done in Formula 1. I was therefore confident that if any car was to get into any difficulty, pretty well on any area of the circuit, as much as humanly possible had been done to cover security. I felt comfortable that the organizers had done a really good job.

I remember saying in a press conference before the race meeting even began that I was optimistic about my prospects for the race. I hoped I'd be competitive but I also realized I was under a lot of pressure simply because of the fact it was my first race and all eyes were on me. There's no question

I went into that race a marked man. I think everybody and their dog wanted to beat me! Coming from Formula 1 as the reigning world champion, there were a lot of great drivers out there gunning for me. Unfortunately it goes with the territory.

That didn't worry me. Winning any race gives you the most fabulous feeling of accomplishment, and in the Indy Car series there are probably at least 10 or 12 drivers who have a legitimate chance to beat me at any particular race. I certainly wasn't expecting any favours. I knew I would get into some situations that I wasn't used to, perhaps be surprised at what some people might and might not do, but at the same time I was already waiting for it.

I was as well-prepared as I could be going into that race. It's all part of what I call the professional approach. What I tried to do – and again the team was very helpful in arranging this for me – was to view tapes of all the races over the last couple of years. I studied a lot of them; in fact I think I watched something like fifty hours of Indy Car races prior to travelling out to Australia. From that I was able to draw my own mental profile of some of the drivers and make some notes about how things were done and things to watch out for.

Australia, of course, was a fantastic way to start the year. It's a beautiful, beautiful venue and the crowd was phenomenal. They made me feel so much at home. It was almost like racing in England! I had a wonderful weekend and a fantastic result, taking pole position and then winning the race. I also created a little piece of Indy Car history from the point of view that in the 84-year existence of the sport no one as a rookie had ever started from pole and won the race. To stand alone and have that accomplishment is something very special indeed.

Not that it was all plain sailing. There were a couple of interesting moments along the way. First of all I messed up the start and then I was assessed a penalty for a yellow flag infraction – which I didn't actually know about until after the race was over – but everthing panned out in the end. I was on a very steep learning curve in Australia, and on the very last lap I was running out of fuel and only just made it to the finish line. In actual fact I did run out of fuel – on the slowing-down lap. I couldn't believe my luck. So for me it was a fairytale start. It was magnificent.

Then we went to Phoenix. The less said about that probably the better! My first ever experience of an oval for a race weekend did not go at all as I'd planned or hoped. Exactly the opposite, in fact, because I had a huge accident. Talk about going from the sublime to the ridiculous: I went from the elation of a history-making victory at Surfers Paradise to punching a hole in the wall at Phoenix. It was pretty hard to deal with.

We were quick in practice and everything seemed to be going well; but then it all went wrong. I really don't remember much about the accident other than it hurt! The car had felt good. It was solid, it was stable and then all of a sudden I was going backwards. At about 180 miles-an-hour. There wasn't anything I could do except just duck my head and hang on. The next thing I knew was about half-an-hour later when I was in the helicopter on the way to the hospital. In a lot of pain.

There's no doubt about it: ovals are a very different science, and as I found out to my cost, you can get bitten very easily. There's no bale-out;

Playing with the dolphins at the Surfers Paradise Sea World. This was one of the most astonishing feelings in the world. Here you can see me being thrown in the air by Slim and his mate. By the way, Slim's the one closest to my heel.

Track food, Phoenix-style.

there's nowhere to go when things go wrong. It tends to put you off a bit, I must admit, although as a professional racing driver that was something I just had to put out of my mind.

I went home to Florida the following day and I was delighted my team-mate Mario was able to win the race – his first victory in almost five years – but I have to say I had other things on my mind. I had an incredible amount of bruising and internal bleeding, and really it wasn't until I got to the next race at Long Beach, California, two weeks later, that I realized how much trouble I was in. It was difficult just getting in and out of the car. The team did everything they could to try to alleviate my problems, but every time the car went over a bump I was quite literally in agony. Every day the doctors were having to drain a large amount of fluid – a pint or more – out of the cavity that had formed in the lower part of my back. It wasn't a pretty sight, I can tell you.

But then to gain pole position with the incredible pain I was enduring was immensely gratifying. I think Long Beach was one of the most difficult and trying races I have ever driven, so after experiencing gearbox problems and losing second gear during the second half of the race, I was just over the moon to finish third. It was more than I could possibly have hoped for.

As soon as I got home, Rosanne and I realized we needed to have something done about my back. Fortunately we had a few weeks off before Indianapolis, so my doctors recommended I undergo surgery to repair the cavity in my back which was responsible for all the internal bleeding. There wasn't time to go through all the convalescence and recuperation that I really needed after such a major operation, which involved more than 100 internal stitches, because I had to try to prepare myself for Indianapolis. That was tough. I had to go through my Rookie Test and then there was time only for a couple of days practice before I had to go out and qualify. We did that all inside three days. It was a bit hectic to say the least, so I was very, very satisfied and pleased to get up to speed as quickly as we did.

For those five or six days after the operation I had never ever laid so still in a bed in my life – because I was petrified of tearing the stitches in my

The Lincoln Mark 8, a great vehicle.

Above The Long Beach circuit is quite different to how I knew it in the Formula 1 days but it's always a great place to visit. The *Queen Mary* still presides majestically over the harbour, although the 'Spruce Goose', Howard Hughes' monster seaplane, has been moved from the adjacent white domed hangar. It has been bought by the father of young Indy Car racer Mark Smith.

Right Winning pole at Long Beach was one of the highlights of my career. I was in a lot of pain. It was very uncomfortable in the car . . . and I must admit I clipped the wall a couple of times on my quickest lap.

One of the best victories ever. It was wonderful to win my first oval mile, which emulated Jimmy Clark's victory of 30 years before.

back. If that had happened it would have meant having open surgery. I didn't even want to contemplate all the possible complications that might have caused. So for once I just did exactly what I was told and hoped I would heal well enough to enable me to do the job at hand.

What with that worry and my crash at Phoenix, my confidence was hit pretty hard. But, thanks to the professionalism of the people at Indianapolis, USAC, the doctors and the Newman-Haas team I was able to get back on my feet again, so to speak, quite quickly. I was pleased with the way everything went. I mean, we could've won the race! It was only through a bit of inexperience and a bit of bad luck that we didn't. If Lyn St James hadn't stalled in the pit lane, the last yellow flag wouldn't have come out and I'm sure we would've won. But that's history now. I finished third and was absolutely delighted with that.

Less than a week later we were in Milwaukee, Wisconsin, which was a completely different kettle of fish. It's a mile oval and very bumpy. Totally different again to anywhere I'd been before, and to start with I really didn't

Paul Tracy is fast developing into a potential champion under the tutelage of four-time Indy 500 winner Rick Mears. Here he is on the podium at Long Beach with Bobby Rahal and me. I was pleased with third place.

know what to think about the place. Qualifying didn't go too well, so I only started seventh, but I managed to pick up the pace and everything came together for the race. I was able gradually to work my way to the front, taking the lead from Raul Boesel in the late stages and then going on to win – in my first ever actual start on a one-mile oval. What a turnaround from Phoenix!

I was also able to create another little bit of history, equalling Jimmy Clark's record of 30 years earlier when he won on his debut at Milwaukee. That was a very special feeling and made me very proud. And I was only able to do that because of the team. They were fantastic. The pit stops were perfect and everything went exactly the way we wanted it to.

Unlike Formula 1, in Indy Car racing it doesn't really matter where you qualify as long as you have a good race car and a good crew. The key is just to keep plugging away – as we proved at Milwaukee.

The next stop was Detroit, where I was again able to put together what I considered to be a great qualifying lap. I was very, very pleased indeed because my Kmart/Havoline Lola was the only Ford/Cosworth-powered car in the top eight on the grid. All the others were Chevrolets.

The race track on Belle Isle, Detroit, is picturesque, but there's no room for overtaking and the surface is prone to breaking up.

An ignominious exit for my Newman-Haas Lola in Detroit.

Unfortunately the race didn't go so well. It was a very indifferent race, a very disappointing race. First of all I was jumped by the two Penskes at the start, then Stefan Johansson hit me from behind while the yellow flags were being waved to warn us about another incident. That effectively put me out of the running, or at least out of contention for the win. Then later as if adding insult to injury I was pushed off line going into a corner by one of the wrecker trucks. That might not have been too bad on its own, except that the racing surface was badly broken up. As soon as I got off onto the 'marbles', that was it. I was history. I hit the wall.

The race track on Belle Isle is quite a good one, well laid out in a very picturesque parkland venue, but there's absolutely no room for passing at all. Also, as I say, the track began to break up in many of the corners. It was very hot that weekend, but the biggest problem was the big heavy Trans-Am cars which really took their toll on the surface. By the time we went out on the track, the damage was done. In this day and age there really isn't much excuse for that. When the surface comes apart, you can't even use the actual racing line. You have to give yourself another couple of feet inside the racing line because if you slide too much you get on the marbles and you're history – even without the help of a wrecker truck.

From 'Motor City' it was on to Portland, Oregon, on the scenic West Coast. It was the seventh race of the PPG Cup season and my very first visit to a 'real' race track, the sort on which I had been brought up in Europe. Portland is a beautiful race track, one that I really enjoyed being at. The facilities are good and there's a golf course at the bottom end of the circuit which is absolutely first-class. The track is situated close to the confluence of two large rivers, the Columbia and the Willamette, and there

This picture shows how scenic Portland International Raceway is.

Below I had to drive very hard to stay ahead of the Penskes during the early laps at Portland. Here I am hotly pursued by Emerson Fittipaldi and Stefan Johansson.

are three huge mountains, all snow-capped even at the end of June, which stand out against the blue sky. It's an incredible sight, especially Mount Hood, which you can see quite clearly as you're coming down the back straight. It makes for a spectacular panoramic view.

The race was very exciting because we had different kinds of weather to contend with. The Penskes were really up to speed at this race and I was delighted to split them on the podium. I was well pleased to finish second. My Formula 1 experience definitely helped me there, because I decided to stay out on slick tyres when almost everyone else came in for wets as soon as it started to rain. Without that I would have finished third, not second.

Cleveland was much the same story. Once again the Penskes were totally dominant. They were much faster than the Lolas, so I was happy to be third. It was fun because I had a great dice with Emerson Fittipaldi towards the end of the race – although it would have been more fun if I'd won! Aside from that, I think it made for a very entertaining race and everybody seemed to appreciate it.

The track itself is a curious place. Burke Lakefront Airport is a fully operational airfield for 362 days of the year and we take it over for just one weekend. It's situated close to the downtown area and right on the edge of Lake Erie. The circuit is quite bumpy on the runways and taxiways but not too bad, and the wide straights really lend themselves to overtaking. In fact Cleveland has a lot going for it because all the grandstands are situated down one side of the track so the spectactors can see virtually every inch of the action from their seats.

Next was Toronto: an accident waiting to happen! The track is not too

I led for a few laps in Cleveland when I out-braked Paul Tracy into the first corner, but I was fighting a losing battle. Quite simply, the Penske team had a better car that weekend.

bad – at least it didn't break up – but it's very difficult to get to grips with because the surface offers very little adhesion. We had an absolutely disastrous weekend. Let's just say the handling was terrible and leave it at that! The race itself wasn't much better because we had a problem with the wastegate, so I didn't finish. But really there was no complaint from my point of view because it was our first mechanical problem of the entire year.

Looking at it from the positive side, the weekend started out badly and finished badly; but at least we got all of that out of the way in one fell swoop! So we just tried to forget about Toronto and put it down to 'That's motor racing'. You have to be prepared to take the rough with the smooth in this business.

Talking about smooth, that certainly isn't the way to describe our next venue, Michigan International Speedway. I'd never seen anything like it. M.I.S. is a two-mile high-banked race track which is flat out all the way around. It has to be one of the quickest race tracks in the world – although I

Toronto was a nightmare weekend. Everything that could have gone wrong did go wrong. Finally I went out of the race with a broken turbo wastegate.

gather Talladega Superspeedway in Alabama, NASCAR stock car country, down in the South, is quite a bit faster. It has similarly high banking but it's quite a bit longer at 2.66 miles. I'm not sure I'd like to take an Indy car around there; I think I'll leave that to one of my own heroes, Dale Earnhardt, who, incidentally, I was fortunate enough to meet during the Marlboro 500 weekend. Great guy. A real racer. I was impressed.

I wasn't quite so impressed with the track at MIS. In fact I wasn't happy, no question about it. It's not much fun going round corners at 230-odd miles-an-hour, especially when you hit huge bumps in the middle of them. Your teeth rattle every time you hit them. It's horrible. But I was more worried about whether the car was going to hold together. All you can do is thank the good Lord and everybody else, especially the designers, that everything held together. It says a lot for the integrity of the cars.

Michigan also hammered home once again what a fabulous team I'm with. It just showed the great strength and depth of the Newman-Haas team. After the fiasco at Toronto, to come back as strongly as we did at Michigan was just fantastic. I was so proud to win my second ever 500-mile race – and on a track I had never seen before Thursday – especially with the bumps and the banking. It was just an astonishing experience.

Even I was surprised to win in what was only my second ever super-speed-way oval race – and I could have won the other one, too, with a little bit of luck – but I'm still not comfortable on the ovals. There's so much to learn. On Saturday night after qualifying, a fan came up to me and said in twenty years of watching at Michigan, he'd never seen anyone take the lines I was taking through the turns. That's because I was still learning – learning how best to avoid the worst of the bumps! It's no easy matter, especially at close to 240 mph.

At the end of the race, I was beat. I had caught some kind of gastric 'bug' during the week and I was up from two to four o'clock in the morning on Friday with, let's say, a distinctly upset tummy. It was not pleasant. As a result of that I hadn't eaten much all weekend and I was severely dehydrated by the end of the race. I lost eight pounds in weight.

Furthermore, because of the bumps and my own anxiety, especially in the early part of the race, I had no comfort zone. I was hanging onto the steering wheel so tight it was draining me of energy. No doubt about it I was having a torrid time. And really it all stems back to the physical problems I've had to contend with all year long. It's frustrating because I know I should be stronger. I've been playing catch-up and I'm just not used to that. For virtually all the season I've been nowhere near my fittest condition.

I'm sure some people will put it down to 'whingeing' but they might conveniently forget what I've been through this year. Even forgetting the gastric problem, ever since the surgery I've had no opportunity to train or build up my strength because I've been on the circuit the whole time. As my specialist told me, normally, when you're fit and healthy, these little things don't bother you too much; but I've been fighting fitness all along. My body can't cope with all the other distractions. Most people, I'm told, wouldn't be back at work for three months after the surgery I had. But I was back in a car in two weeks, so considering all that, I'm absolutely delighted with the way things have gone.

I was even more delighted the following weekend. The bad news was

Above The parade lap at Michigan International Speedway. One more lap to the green flag.

Left Michigan was a resounding success for the Newman-Haas team with Mario winning pole and then following me home in the race. Arie Luyendyk also drove well to finish third.

Opposite Thumbs up after winning the Marlboro 500; but boy, 250 laps around that place and you know you've done a day's work. That was tough!

that I 'celebrated' my fortieth birthday, but the good news was that I was able to do so with another win – on an absolutely superb race track. New Hampshire International Speedway is an altogether different kind of oval to the others I had already visited. It's fractionally over a mile in length and with relatively long straights and tight corners.

I think most people tend to presume all the one-mile ovals are very similar. They're not. They are very, very different. As different as Silverstone is to Brands Hatch, or Le Mans is to Monza. Comparing Milwaukee with Phoenix or New Hampshire is like comparing chalk with cheese.

New Hampshire is a great circuit. It's very exciting, it's very smooth – a welcome contrast to Michigan – and it's very busy out there. You have to deal with a lot in just 22 seconds, which is about how long it takes to complete a lap.

The facility itself is absolutely first-class and it's set in quite beautiful New England countryside which really did remind me of home. I ended up having a fabulous race with Paul Tracy and Emerson Fittipaldi. It was cut and thrust, nip and tuck the whole way. It was like a high-speed game of chess because you had to anticipate what the other guys were going to do, especially when we got in amongst the traffic.

Afterwards Paul described it as white-knuckle racing for the last ten laps or so. Ten laps? More like the whole 200 laps from my perspective! It was pure, thoroughbred racing at its very, very best. I've been in some exciting races before; I've been wheel-to-wheel with Ayrton Senna at 200 mph, but even that doesn't come close to the race we had at New Hampshire. It was yet another incredible experience in an incredible year.

Opposite The yellow flags are out at New Hampshire and everyone takes the opportunity to make a pit stop. My Newman-Haas crew was flawless as ever.

Opposite below Birthday boy at New Hampshire. The hat says it all: 'I look 30, act 20, feel like 60, I must be 40!' The best present on the day of course was the win.

Below If anyone, anywhere in the world, is seriously considering construction of an oval track, New Hampshire International Speedway should be the model. It's a super facility. There is also a road course which uses a portion of the infield as well as more ground outside the back straight.

As to the remaining races, who knows what might happen? I haven't a clue about Road America or Vancouver – except I'm told they're both very good race tracks. Road America is situated an hour or so north of Milwaukee, just outside the summer resort village of Elkhart Lake, Wisconsin, which is in the heart of America's dairy land. The Vancouver layout is a fast street circuit which circumnavigates B.C. Place stadium in the largest city on the West Coast of Canada.

Nazareth is yet another variation on the one-mile oval theme in that it comprises three distinct and very different corners. We're due to go testing there in preparation for the race.

Mid-Ohio is also somewhere we've tested. It's a very, very nice course, quite similar to Oulton Park in that it winds through a beautiful parkland setting, but again I think it's going to be a very difficult place for overtaking. It's also a track on which it will be critical to get the car set up well. So much so, in fact, that we're planning to squeeze in another test there before the race.

We then finish up at Laguna Seca, which is where I came in a year ago for my first visit to an Indy Car race. It's a fabulous circuit, twisting and turning its way around the coastal hills only a few miles away from Monterey Bay and the Pacific Ocean. Laguna is a thoroughbred professional venue and the perfect place to round off the season.

One thing for certain is that there's an incredible variety among the race tracks. The constant transitions from one type of a track to another certainly make it difficult for anyone to maintain an edge over the rest of the opposition and I think that probably helps to keep the cars and drivers fairly evenly matched. If I look down the list of regular entrants it's not difficult to see why the series has become as strong as it has. There are some very good drivers and teams involved.

There's no question as to whom I regard as the number one threat this year. It's Emerson Fittipaldi and the Penske team. The reason is purely and simply that they are the works team for Chevrolet engines and the team builds its own chassis, designed by Nigel Bennett. They have their own wind-tunnel programme and it goes without saying anything they find to help the car, no one else has access to. They are extremely competitive in '93 and it's going to be a great challenge to keep pace with the Penske team both mechanically and aerodynamically. Their operation is second to none. They are to Indy Car what McLaren or Williams are to Formula 1.

Emerson, who won the Formula 1 World Championship in 1972 and 1974, and also won the PPG Cup title in 1989 as well as twice winning the Indianapolis 500, is rejuvenated by the position in which he finds himself at the Penske organization. He's hungry. He's very, very fit. He likes this type of racing. He loves the car he's driving because it's a very good one and he's been and done it all before. So there are no surprises for Emerson and it's no surprise to me that he's the man I have to beat. At the end of the year, he's going to be there or thereabouts.

Emerson's teammate Paul Tracy is a young fired-up charger. He may make the occasional mistake but he is extremely quick and obviously talented. We'll see in due course how he matures: he could be very strong.

Robby Gordon, who drives for the team owned by A. J. Foyt, is in the same pigeon hole – except Robby Gordon is less experienced than Paul

Emerson Fittipaldi may be 46 years old but he's driving as well as ever. He's always tough to beat.

Robby Gordon, one of the stars of tomorrow, exiting his car quickly due to engine failure.

Opposite Al Unser Jr. has not had a good season but he's always likely to bounce back into contention. He's a good, talented, hard-charging driver.

Tracy. He's done less mileage and because of that has more to learn. I believe that Robby has the makings of a very talented driver but he needs to pay attention to the straight-talking guidance that I'm sure he gets from A.J.

Scott Goodyear is a great talent on some circuits. I'm just surprised that he's not more consistent with Derrick Walker's team. It seems to be a case of horses for courses. He's a good racer. If he likes the track he's extremely competitive; if he doesn't like the track or more likely he has a problem with the car then he's off the pace.

These three are regarded as the 'young lions' of Indy Car racing right now. Against them is a veritable who's who of experienced and talented champions. Take my own teammate, Mario Andretti, for example. Obviously he's extremely accomplished. Mario has won just about everything there is to win in this sport, including the 1978 Formula 1 World Championship and four Indy Car championships. He's won the Indianapolis 500 and the Daytona 500 stock car race. In his heyday he was second to none, on a par with the best there has ever been. Last year in America he was voted, quite rightly, as the Driver of the Quarter-Century. Now in the later stages of his career, he's still there, still a threat but not as competitive as he used to be. But always a competitor.

Two of Mario's contemporaries were brothers Al and Bobby Unser. Al's son, Al Jr., is now one of the top Indy Car drivers and has been so for several years. He won the Championship in 1990 and although he is rarely at the front in qualifying he is a hard charger and – come the race – is always a competitor to be reckoned with, having a tremendous will to win.

Danny Sullivan is very, very professional. He loves his job and he's very good at it, but his performance can vary a lot from track to track.

Raul Boesel, is, I believe, very talented. He was underrated in Formula 1 some years ago and he's yet to win an Indy Car race, but he's a very serious competitor.

Perhaps the smartest, shrewdest driver of them all is Bobby Rahal. He's very clever and a thorough professional. Bobby has put together a very strong team. He's always competitive and a very quick driver at times, but not the quickest. The way he plans his races and packages the team and manages the car is very astute. He's won three PPG championships and you don't do that if you don't know what you're doing. Bobby is also an avid golfer!

Chip Ganassi's driver, Arie Luyendyk, is one of the most likeable people on the circuit. I think he's a great personality but his strengths seem to vary from circuit to circuit. On some tracks he's incredibly quick, very competitive, and at other times one wonders what's happened. Arie's always a star on the ovals yet rarely a force on the road courses, which is strange because his background was all on road circuits.

Eddie Cheever is another one who's quick sometimes and not others which surprises me in view of his great talent. But Eddie's American-Italian. I think that says a lot. He's very fiery at times but his achievements haven't been as consistent as he must have hoped. I suppose I have been fortunate that I have been able to maintain my competitiveness while Eddie's only surfaces occasionally. He has been without a regular drive this year but has returned for some late season races and is working on a deal to return for next year.

One man that has returned this season after some time away is Teo Fabi. Again when motivated he can be very quick, very competitive, but he rarely seems to get fired up. Teo is a nice, quiet Italian gentleman. He's an incredibly experienced and talented driver but he must be disappointed he hasn't won more than he has.

It really is a strong field. Not only that but the future looks very bright indeed. The sport is just growing and growing. I think for Indy Car racing itself that's fabulous. There's talk of Honda and maybe Toyota coming in with new engines, and Reynard – another British racing car constructor – has announced it will attempt to challenge Lola's share of the customer chassis marketplace.

Rather more exciting as far as I'm concerned is the possible expansion of the series into different overseas arenas. I know there is serious talk of a race at Brands Hatch, or at least somewhere in Europe, and perhaps also in Japan or Mexico. I think for the series – as long as the meat of the racing continues to be held in America – if you have two, three or four races outside America it has to help the overall picture. There is a lot of interest in the series throughout the world right now, and that seems set only to increase. That in turn should help attract sponsorship, and as the exposure increases, so everybody benefits.

For the Indy Car scene, the upward spiral of success has just started spinning . . .

Danny Sullivan, the 1988 PPG Cup champion, scored an upset win in Detroit for the Galles Racing International team.

Above opposite Raul Boesel has done a tremendous job this season for Dick Simon's team but in August still seeks his first victory.

Above far right Eddie Cheever (*left*) and Morris Nunn are two well-known faces from the Formula 1 days. In 1992 they were together on the same team. This year Eddie contested only the first few races before running out of finance. Morris has continued as race engineer with Chip Ganassi's team which now enters Arie Luyendyk.

Opposite On the podium at Milwaukee.

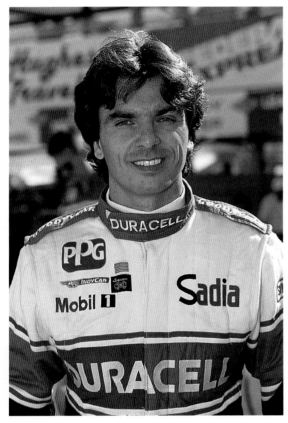

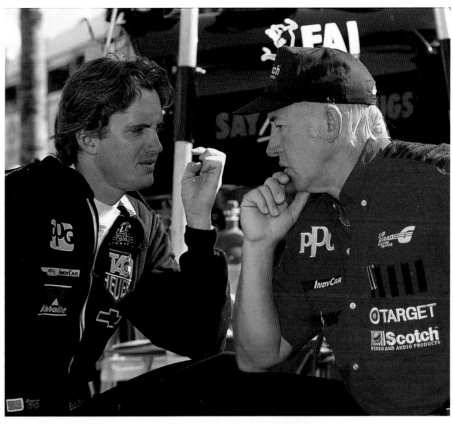

147

Road America, Elkhart Lake, Wisconsin. One of the more important races of the year to finish. The circuit reminds me of a blend of the Osterreichring in Austria and Brands Hatch; it's very challenging and demanding.

A-Z
of Indy Car Terms

Above Special arrangements were made with the PPG Championship organisers for me to keep the lucky number five of my Formula 1 days.

A glossary of terms and names commonplace around the Indy Car scene, with which I have had to become familiar while opening a new chapter in my racing career:

Aluminum	American spelling of aluminium.
Andretti	Along with the Unsers the top dynasty in Indy Car racing; my teammate is 1978 World Champion Mario Andretti. Sons Michael (now competing in F1) and Jeff, and nephew John are accomplished racers.
Banking	The incline across the race track in a corner on an oval.
Brickyard	The Indianapolis Motor Speedway (Indy), so called because it was first paved in 1909 with more than three million bricks.
CART	Championship Auto Racing Teams, sanctioning body of the PPG Indy Car World Series (see also USAC).
Checker	The chequered flag.
Drafting	Slipstreaming.
ECU	Electronic Control Unit, not the European Currency Unit.
Emmo	Nickname for two-time F1 World Champion Emerson Fittipaldi, who also won the 1989 PPG Indy Car World Series crown.
Foyt	A.J., the doyen of Indy Car racing.
Gas	Gasoline, or petrol; also used to describe the accelerator pedal.
Gas-and-go	A quick pit stop for a splash of fuel, usually in the closing stages of a race.
Groove	The racing line through a corner, especially on the ovals (eg 'in the groove' or 'high groove').
Hole shot	Drag racing term: getting a jump start.
Hot lap	A lap at speed; a qualifying lap.
Indy	The Indianapolis Motor Speedway.
Indy 500	'The 500', comprising 200 laps around the 2.5 mile Indianapolis Motor Speedway – the jewel in the series' crown.
Junior	Second-generation driver (eg Al Unser Jr.).
Kmart	Discount department store, major sponsor with Texaco/Havoline of the Newman-Haas team.

Loose	Oversteer; where the rear of the car feels as though it's trying to overtake the front.
Lyn St James	Female racer – 1992 Indianapolis 500 Rookie of the Year.
Methanol	Grain-derived Indy car fuel, less volatile than petrol, burns with an invisible flame.
'Murrican	Pronunciation of anything pertaining to the US.
Nail it	'Jump on the gas (pedal).'
Nerf	Nudge; to bump wheels.
Oval	Circuit featuring a continuous left-hand bend; examples in many shapes and sizes.
Pace car	Safety car used to pace the field before the start and following on-course incidents.
Pit lizard	Groupie; especially good-looking female of the species, commonly found in the pit and paddock areas.
Pop-off valve	A mandatory device used to regulate manifold boost pressure (and therefore horsepower) on turbocharged Indy car.
PPG	Automotive Finishes Group of PPG Industries, title sponsor of the Indy Car World Series.
Purse	Prize money. The Indy winner earns more than $1 million.
Push	Understeer; opposite of 'loose'.
Qualifying	Referred to in Europe as 'official practice', when grid places are established; on an oval, cars take to the track one at a time.
Rookie	A first year Indy Car driver (eg me!).
Speedway	The Speedway – Indianapolis.
Stagger	Differing rolling circumference of the rear tyres, used on oval to aid cornering.
Stop-and-go	Penalty assessed for pit or other infraction, requires driver to stop at his pit, then resume.
Straightaway	Straight.
Tech	Technical inspection; scrutineering.
Tire	Not fatigue, just American for tyre.
Tri-Oval	Three-cornered oval such as Nazareth or Michigan Internation Speedway.
Turn	Corner.
Unser	Three family members, Bobby, Al and Al Jr., have eight Indianapolis 500 wins between them.
USAC	United States Auto Club, which, uniquely, sanctions the Indianapolis 500.
Vaughn	Linda, the ultimate pit lizard – a much admired fixture at most Indy Car races.
Wrench	Spanner; also used to describe a mechanic.
X	Used to designate spare chassis; called 'T' (for training) car in Formula 1.
Yellows	Full course caution – no overtaking allowed.
Zip	Zero, the number of Indy Car races I had seen in my life prior to Laguna Seca at the end of '92.

Indy Car Champions

1909–1992

Based on official AAA-USAC-IndyCar records

AAA

1909	George Robertson
1910	Ray Harroun
1911	Ralph Mulford
1912	Ralph DePalma
1913	Earl Cooper
1914	Ralph DePalma
1915	Earl Cooper
1916	Dario Resta
1917	Earl Cooper
1918	Ralph Mulford
1919	Howard Wilcox
1920	Tommy Milton (11 races)
1921	Gaston Chevrolet (5 races)
1922	Jimmy Murphy
1923	Eddie Hearne
1924	Jimmy Murphy
1925	Peter DePaolo
1926	Harry Hartz
1927	Peter DePaolo
1928	Louis Meyer
1929	Louis Meyer
1930	Billy Arnold
1931	Louis Schneider
1932	Bob Carey
1933	Louis Meyer
1934	Bill Cummings
1935	Kelly Petillo
1936	Mauri Rose
1937	Wilbur Shaw
1938	Floyd Roberts
1939	Wilbur Shaw
1940	Rex Mays
1941	Rex Mays
1942–6	no racing
1947	Ted Horn
1948	Ted Horn
1949	Johnnie Parsons
1950	Henry Banks
1951	Tony Bettenhausen
1952	Chuck Stevenson
1953	Sam Hanks
1954	Jimmy Bryan
1955	Bob Sweikert

USAC

1956	Jimmy Bryan
1957	Jimmy Bryan
1958	Tony Bettenhausen
1959	Rodger Ward
1960	A.J. Foyt Jr.
1961	A.J. Foyt Jr.
1962	Rodger Ward
1963	A.J. Foyt Jr.
1964	A.J. Foyt Jr.
1965	Mario Andretti
1966	Mario Andretti
1967	A.J. Foyt Jr.
1968	Bobby Unser
1969	Mario Andretti
1970	Al Unser
1971	Joe Leonard
1972	Joe Leonard
1973	Roger McCluskey
1974	Bobby Unser
1975	A.J. Foyt Jr.
1976	Gordon Johncock
1977	Tom Sneva
1978	Tom Sneva
1979	A.J. Foyt Jr.

INDYCAR

1979	Rick Mears
1980	Johnny Rutherford
1981	Rick Mears
1982	Rick Mears
1983	Al Unser
1984	Mario Andretti
1985	Al Unser
1986	Bobby Rahal
1987	Bobby Rahal
1988	Danny Sullivan
1989	Emerson Fittipaldi
1990	Al Unser Jr.
1991	Michael Andretti
1992	Bobby Rahal

Index

Acknowledgements

Jeremy Shaw would like to thank several people without whose considerable assistance and encouragement this project could not have been completed. Among them are Steve Nickless and Paul Oxman who first afforded me the opportunity to move to America; Gordon Kirby for introducing me to so many people in the early days; Paul Pfanner, David Phillips and Rick Shatter for being good friends and helping in hours of need; Donald Davidson for knowing everything there is to possibly know about USAC and Indianapolis; Emma Way for remaining unflustered in times of stress (especially when my copy was late); and Tamy Valkosky for helping to preserve my sanity, transcribing the tapes and reading manuscripts into the wee hours.

PHOTOGRAPHIC ACKNOWLEDGEMENTS

The publishers would like to thank the following for their kind permission to reproduce the photographs listed below:
MICHAEL BROWN 47, 51, 57, 134, 135, 137, 148–9
INDY 500 PHOTOS, INDIANAPOLIS MOTOR SPEEDWAY CORPORATION 21, 24, 25, 27, 28 top, 30, 33, 34, 37, 39 top and bottom, 41, 43 top and bottom, 45, 99, 101
STEVE SWOPE RACING PHOTOS 136 top and bottom